PLAYING BALL
WITH THE BOYS

The Rise of Women in the World of Men's Sports

Betsy M. Ross
Former ESPN Anchor
Foreword by Phyllis George

CLERISY PRESS

Playing Ball with the Boys:
The Rise of Women in the World of Men's Sports

Published by Clerisy Press
Distributed by Publishers Group West
Printed in the United States of America
First edition, first printing

Editor: Jack Heffron
Cover Design: Scott McGrew
Text Design: Annie Long

Library of Congress Cataloging-in-Publication Data
    Ross, Betsy M.
        Playing ball with the boys : the rise of women in the world of
            men's sports / by Betsy M. Ross.
        p. cm.
        ISBN-13: 978-1-57860-460-9 (pbk.); ISBN-10: 1-57860-460-5
        ISBN 978-1-57860-461-6 (ebook); ISBN 978-1-57860-620-7 (hardcover)
        1. Sports for women--United States. 2. Women athletes--
        United States. I. Title.

        GV709.18.U6R67 2010
        796.082--dc22   2010020563

CLERISY PRESS
An imprint of AdventureKEEN
306 Greenup Street
Covington, KY 41011
clerisypress.com

TO MY PARENTS

*Who always told me I could be,
and do, anything I wanted*

contents

acknowledgments

I didn't realize it at the time, but it seems as if I've always had this book in me.

As I started the research into the women who have made a difference in sports, I found that I already had a lot of the material in my files: Clippings of the *New York Times* article on Gayle Sierens; columns from *USA Today's* Christine Brennan; research articles on why more women weren't involved more in such-and-such aspect of athletics. There are many people to thank who helped me get this book out of my files, out of my head, and onto paper.

The inherent fear, of course, is that you won't name everyone who has played a part in this project, like the Oscar-winning actress who forgets to name her spouse. So if your name isn't here, please don't think of it as an oversight, or a slight of any kind. I just have had so many people who have helped me develop this book and this research, that it may be nearly impossible to list everyone who has touched my life.

First, of course, are the many women who have gone before us in the field of sports and made a difference. I've had the opportunity to interview a number in this book, but there are many more, be they famous or anonymous, who have worked to make it better for the next generation. Those with whom I had the privilege to talk were gracious to give their time and were eager to tell their stories, and I thank them.

Knowing to whom you want to talk is one thing; actually finding them is another. That's where these people come in: Jeremy Martin in the University of Cincinnati sports communications office; Mollie Busam from Impact Basketball Academy; Dana Rieger, director of basketball operations for the University of Cincinnati women's basketball team; Michael Anderson from the Cincinnati Reds; Don North, WFLA, Tampa; Rebecca Cox, Nationwide Racing; the Association for Women in Sports Media for its research and member networking; Robin Gehl, Kevin Reynolds, and the staff at WVXU-FM for letting me conduct many of these interviews for my "Front Row" radio interview segment; Vicki Blackwell Morrison for your encouragement and your contacts; Joe Jareck from the Los Angeles Dodgers; Bill Tavares, media relations manager for the WNBA's Connecticut Sun; and Bill Keating. Your help made these amazing interviews possible, and I thank you for your information and your contacts.

Those who encouraged my pursuit of a profession in sports also deserve a nod, including the sports staff at the *South Bend Tribune* who gave me my first sports break and let me cover high school sports while I was working on my master's degree; Phil Lengyel, my first news director at WSJV-TV, who let me fill in for the sports anchor and fueled my dreams of doing it full time; Darrel Burnett, my colleague at WTHR-TV in Indianapolis, who got a job as a sports anchor at Sports Channel America and suggested I do the same (which I did); the staff at NBC NewsChannel, who gave me the amazing assignment to cover the Olympic trials and 1996 Olympics in Atlanta; Al Jaffe, who gave me the opportunity of a lifetime at ESPN, and Pat Casey (and later Steve Ackermann), the news directors at WXIX-TV in Cincinnati, who continue to keep me involved in sports. Each of you has played a role in helping me pursue my passion.

Next, thanks to my unofficial posse of "editors," including Jackie Reau, Suzanne Vanderhoef, and Dr. Linda Schoenstedt. Anyone who works on a project knows you can get a little too close and a little too possessive, and they were able to give me perspective. Their writing and editing skills went a long way in the construction of this book.

. . .

Thanks as well to the real editor of the book, Jack Heffron at Clerisy Press. He was the one who looked at my idea and envisioned its possibilities. I saw a small business book, but Jack saw a book that could have a much wider reach. He helped me broaden my expectations of what I could do and those I could reach with it. I appreciate his vision and his guidance in making this possible.

And while my mother encouraged my love of sports, my teachers encouraged my passion for writing. Mrs. Crawford and Miss Brantley at Connersville High School taught me to write to my own style and spell correctly (most of the time), and Mrs. Lee gave me my first opportunity to see my name and columns in print in the high school newspaper, the *Clarion*. I'll never forget the thrill of seeing my first byline.

None of this could have been possible without all of you and your support. I thank you, and the young women and girls who I hope will be inspired by this book. Thank you.

foreword

$\mathcal{P}$hyllis George is one of the best-known Miss Americas and became a familiar face even before she began her television career. Her broadcasting skills are legendary from entertainment to news to sports and make her one of the most successful women broadcasters of all time. From guest spots on late-night television to co-hosting *Candid Camera* with Allen Funt and the Miss America Pageant with Bert Parks, she caught the eye of the late Robert Wussler, then vice president of CBS Sports, who convinced her to join CBS Sports in 1974. Her interviews and feature stories were the first to show viewers the personal side of athletes—and led her to the set of *The NFL Today* after covering many sports and interviewing basketball stars, tennis stars, and more. She became co-host of CBS's *The NFL Today* in 1975. Her work on the groundbreaking pregame show helped other women break into sports media, and her interviews helped The NFL Today win multiple Emmys and become the best sports show of its time. Though she was the first woman in this all-male fraternity, she didn't allow the bumps to get in the way of a successful ten-year run at CBS Sports.

She has enjoyed success in a variety of national roles as an author, inspirational speaker, entrepreneur, and in politics as the First Lady of Kentucky. But it's her time with CBS that made her one of the best-known pioneers for women in sports broadcasting and paved the way for women to be included in NFL coverage. Her work earned her the distinction of being the only female listed in the "50 Greatest Network Announcers" as compiled by David J. Halberstam for Yahoo! Sports. She is in the first class of The Paley Center for Media's "She Made It" initiative, celebrating the achievements of creative women and businesswomen in the industries of television, radio, and new media.

...

The climate now for women sportscasters is a hundred times better than when I started in the '70s and '80s. I look back now and say, "What was I thinking?!"

As I recall those early years—maybe it was my youth—I believed I could do anything and wanted to make a difference.

It's only now and in the last few years that I have realized what I, indeed, did. Maybe that comes with being a "seasoned," more mature person.

I'm a veteran, one of the "firsts." I didn't have time "back in the day" to think much about what was being said about CBS hiring me, or the catty, sometimes mean-spirited comments.

I had a contract—a job to do—so I just put my head down and worked hard. I felt as if I was filling a void in sports, by interviewing and humanizing—personalizing—the athletes. I asked questions the men couldn't ask.

This is important—I NEVER mixed business and pleasure. That would have been the "Kiss of Death."

When you are one of the "firsts"—at anything—there are naysayers and doubters hurling comments at you so fast that you just have to stop reading everything and anything negative.

Once I stopped reading the "reviews," my work was better and the critical comments became fewer and fewer.

Our team on *The NFL Today,* I'm told, was the gold standard, even today, for other pregame shows.

Bob Wussler, a visionary who had the foresight to put together our team—Brent Musburger, Irv Cross, me, and eventually Jimmy the Greek—knew what he was doing.

I did have to deal with the crude comments and rude behavior of Jimmy the Greek. He made my life miserable, but I never talked about it. I just put up with it until one day he really crossed the line and I finally said, "It's either him or me."

We compromised. CBS kept both of us. He taped his piece in the morning and Brent, Irv, and I did the show LIVE. Jimmy's picks were inserted into the live *NFL Today* telecast. At the end, I forgave Jimmy, and we became friends. And all in all, my time on *The NFL Today* at CBS was one of the most rewarding and exciting times in my life.

I am so happy there are more women in the sports world than ever before. But there needs to be more. Even today, it's hard to break into "the old boys club," but we can't give up—never give up.

The woman's perspective must be listened to and read about in sports. Just look at the statistics regarding female fans/participants/viewers: We represent close to 50 percent of all of the above, and we buy three-fourths of everything for the home.

Hopefully the networks will continue to realize this because the advertisers will cater to us—it makes so much sense.

Young girls now have options of what they want to be when they grow up, thanks to all of the pioneers who were there in the beginning.

I'm incredibly proud to have been one of those women who people remember as one of the "first" female sportscasters.

Women power!

introduction

$\mathcal{I}$ can remember exactly where I was when the idea hit me that I wanted to cover sports for a living, and do it on television. While I was in college at South Bend a group of us drove to Chicago to see a White Sox game at old Comiskey Park. Yes, it was old and creaky, but it was like going to old Yankee Stadium or Fenway Park—you could touch the baseball history everywhere. Babe Ruth played there, so did Foxx, Gehrig, any number of American League legends. It smelled of baseball greatness.

Those were the days when you could drive up on an early Saturday evening and get good seats, ten rows up, along the first base line. That's exactly what we did this particular summer evening. As we settled into our seats, the visiting Kansas City Royals' television broadcast team was on the field, doing the pre-game show for the home market.

I watched them do their standups and requisite anchor banter while the teams warmed up behind them, and I thought, "I can do that. I can talk baseball, or basketball, or football before the games, do interviews and the like. There's no reason why I can't do that."

It absolutely never occurred to me that, because I was female, I wouldn't have the chance to cover sports. I just was going on the assumption that, if I was good enough, I'd get the opportunity.

Perhaps that was being more naïve than practical, but by then, we were seeing more women on television and more women covering sports. Now, I grew up during the time when about the only women you would see on TV on a regular basis were on the news: Nancy Dickerson, who covered the White House, and Pauline Frederick at the United Nations for NBC News. Later, Barbara Walters moved across town from *The Today Show* to ABC News. Jane Pauley, from my home state of Indiana, slid into *The Today Show* anchor position.

By the time I was in college, however, more women were covering sports on television, and so it didn't seem like such a farfetched idea that I could do the same. Jane Chastain and Phyllis George were covering sports just about every weekend, and by the time ESPN was on twenty-four hours a day, women were regularly seen on the anchor desk and in the field.

Now, I wish I could tell you that just by thinking I could do it, the doors opened and sports departments welcomed me with open arms. Not quite that easy. It didn't happen overnight, but it eventually happened, mainly because I never thought I couldn't reach that goal. I didn't get there by myself—many people helped me along the way—just like the women in this book were helped as they achieved their dreams.

But one of my great regrets involves a young woman whom I couldn't figure out how to help. When I was student teaching, I had a girl in our journalism class who was an excellent writer. She enjoyed it, you could tell, and had a real talent for expressing herself in her newspaper stories. One day after class I told her that she should think about majoring in journalism in college.

"I'm not planning to go to college," she said. "My dad says girls don't need to go to college, so I'll be done when I get out of high school."

I smiled and told her to keep writing, and maybe she'd have the opportunity to expand her talents in some other way. But frankly, I was speechless. This wasn't the 1800s. This wasn't a Third World country. But this very talented young lady was being told, by someone she respected, that she didn't need to grow, to make herself better, to offer a talent that few people discover and embrace. I don't know if she ever had a chance to write, or to go to college. I regret not figuring out a way to help her. I hope for her sake, and for her family's, that she was able to find a way to use her talents.

And there are still opportunities for education. When we were starting our public relations business, Game Day Communications, our small-business contact at our company bank changed a couple of times in just the few months from when we first signed with them. The third small-business vice president, when he called to introduce himself, started the conversation with me by saying, "Now what is it that you girls do?" Amazing that he could insult us twice in one little sentence—first, by not taking the time to research what our company did, and, second, by calling two businesswomen "girls." It should go without saying that we switched banks rather quickly after that.

One more comment on this theme: The first Super Bowl I attended, XXVIII in Atlanta, I was making some observations on the Dallas offense to the people I was sitting with in the stands, when the gentleman in front, I'd guess in his early forties, turned around and said, "You seem to know a lot about football for a girl." He didn't know I was going to be doing a live wrap-up from the field for my station in Cincinnati once the game was over. I gave him my business card, signed it, and said, "Hang onto that so you'll remember my name." Hope he still has it.

Not long ago I was sitting in a college press box when a young woman in the university's sports information office said to me, "I don't know how you put up with working in sports. The funny looks, being disrespected sometimes—I still hear it, and I'm sure you did, too. It's hard enough now, but I can't imagine how tough it must have been years ago."

Well, years ago, a group of women defied the odds and followed their passions to get into sports—and made it possible for my sports information friend to sit in press boxes and cover games. These are the stories of some of them who were among the first to break through and break barriers. These are the women who were, and still are, "playing ball with the boys."

chapter 1

"This is SportsCenter"

Congratulations, Mrs. Ross, you have a boy!"

Hearing that, my mother immediately broke into tears.

Dr. Gregg took a closer look. "Oops, no, I was wrong, you have another daughter."

That daughter was me.

Now, whether that pronouncement at my birth had any affect on my profession of choice, I'm not sure, but I do know that growing up, my tastes trended more toward baseball than baby dolls—a tomboy, in the vernacular of the day. Not that my parents didn't try to make me more ladylike. One Christmas, I discovered a doll and baby carriage under the tree. I think they're still sitting in the corner

5

of the basement. After that it was cork guns and volleyballs and basketballs. And my parents were wise enough never to dissuade me from what I really enjoyed.

I grew up outside of the town of Connersville, in southeastern Indiana, in a rural area where every home had a basketball hoop and the Cincinnati Reds were the team of choice. I was the typical kid who would fall asleep with the transistor radio under my pillow. I'd even carry it with me in the grocery store when the Reds were playing on Saturday afternoons. And usually, someone would ask me the score of the game.

Since there were few kids my age to play sports with, and my sister, eleven years older than I, was already away in college, my mother was, more often than not, drafted as my playing partner. While Dad was at work at the factory, my mother would pitch batting practice to me or catch the football.

She was no stranger to sports herself—in fact, she would brag about her crooked right pinky, bent at the slightest outside angle, from a softball that came in just a little too fast during recess at Orange Elementary School. So even though her knees hurt and her back was tired, she'd often take a few minutes to keep me occupied in the back yard.

One time, we were playing one-on-one basketball in the gravel driveway in the back and Mom had the ball. She went up for a shot, I reached up to block her, and my hand slammed into her nose. Of course, any time you hit the nose, it gushes blood like a Texas oil strike. I was distraught, but it turned out there was no damage. In telling the story in later years, when people were horrified that I had mugged my mother, I just explained, "Well, she was driving the lane, what else was I supposed to do?" And my basketball friends completely understood.

Now, all of this happened before Title IX, which has given countless young girls the opportunity to play sports in high school and college. So I couldn't understand why I couldn't play Little League baseball with the boys, when I played softball with them during school recess. Or why I couldn't participate in Punt, Pass and Kick competitions when I'd play touch football with the guys during lunch hour. In fact, one of my badges of honor in the seventh grade at Garrison Creek School was having my name written in the back of the grade book—reserved only for serious infractions— for playing touch football after our teacher, Mr. Fowler, told me I couldn't. (By the way, in a remarkable twist of fate, when the Cincinnati Bengals hold the regional Punt, Pass and Kick finals at Paul Brown Stadium each year, I have the privilege of handling the stadium announcements for the competition, introducing each participant—boys AND girls.)

But in school, when I couldn't participate in sports, I did the next best thing—I wrote about sports. I was very fortunate when I was a youngster in that I knew at a fairly early age I wanted to write. I attended a one-room school in our rural area—two of them, in fact, Nulltown for grades one through four and Garrison Creek for grades five through eight—before I went to Connersville High School. I was first published in the sixth grade when I wrote a letter to the editor of the local paper. Now, that was pretty heady stuff, seeing your name in print when you're ten years old!

But that was enough to give me the writing bug. Well, that, and, when I was watching the news, I noticed that President Lyndon

Johnson called NBC News reporter Nancy Dickerson by her first name at news conferences. Wow, that's cool, I thought. Presidents know your name if you're a reporter.

So I decided that was what I wanted to do. I didn't know much about the process of journalism, other than what I read in the paper every day and saw on television. But an assignment from Mr. Fowler at Garrison Creek changed my life. The assignment was: Interview someone. Now, you could interview your friend, your brother, your parents, anyone, and that's what most kids did in my class (all seven of us!). But I decided to interview Candace Murray, the author of the daily "O Yez O Yez" heard-about-town column that was published in the *Connersville News-Examiner* newspaper.

So Mom made the appointment, we waited for Dad to get home from work so he could drive us the seven miles up to town, and Candace waited for us at the *News-Examiner* office so I could do my interview. It's funny, I don't remember a whole lot about the interview itself, but I remember the smells of the newsroom (ink mixed with newsprint) and the stacks of chaos on everyone's desk (old newspapers, letters, copy paper, all of it). I thought it was great.

She gave us a quick tour of the newsroom and the printing area in the back—those huge printing machines like you see in the old movies churning out full pages of printed newspaper. It was fascinating. I was hooked. I knew that was what I wanted to do.

Now, what if she had said no to the interview? Or if she had given me only a half hour of her time instead of staying late at work? I might have been a veterinarian (my second choice of profession) instead of going into journalism. So to this day, I thank Candace Murray for helping me choose journalism—and if a student wants to come by the office for an interview, or to shadow me for a day, I always say yes. You never know when you'll have an influence on someone's life.

So, I took the usual journalism paths, working on the high school newspaper and yearbook, then moving on to Ball State University, partly because of its great journalism program, partly because my sister went there and I was familiar with the campus. Admittedly, I wasn't big on working on the *Ball State Daily News* campus newspaper; with the journalism classes and with extra classes to get my teaching certificate I was busy enough. But I dreamed of taking what I learned and becoming an investigative reporter for the *Chicago Sun-Times*.

But again, one seemingly innocuous decision made a huge difference in my professional life. Since I was working on a teaching certificate, I had to do one quarter of student teaching. I was planning to do it at my old high school, like most people did, so I could live at home and save expenses. As we were setting up my student teaching schedule, my counselor said, "You can do two classes in journalism and two in English." That made sense, since English was my minor, but it was hardly my favorite subject.

"Tell you what," I said. "I really have no plans to teach English. Is there anything else you can give me to teach along with journalism?"

"Well, Connersville High has a radio/TV program," he said. "Do you want to teach two classes in radio and television?"

"Sure," I said. How hard can it be? I thought.

Well, let me tell you, it was harder than I dreamed. Since I had zero, zip classes in radio and television at Ball State, and the

Betsy Ross and former Ohio State women's basketball player Toni Roesch announcing a women's basketball game between the University of Cincinnati and Xavier University.

campus broadcast facilities were not necessarily the best (this was the pre-David Letterman Communication and Media Building days), it never crossed my mind to take broadcast classes. So I'd study whatever the topic was the day before I had to teach it, and do video projects right along with the students.

And I had a blast.

I learned to shoot a video camera, edit, I learned everything about a television studio, writing for TV, and I learned it fast. I thought it was the coolest thing ever. And I also thought, "Great, it's my last quarter of my senior year in college and I finally figure out what I want to do."

After graduation, I landed a job teaching journalism and advising for the yearbook and newspaper at Merrillville High School in Indiana, but I never got the television bug out of my brain. I taught one year, then joined the staff at the *South Bend Tribune*, a terrific newspaper that still serves as the paper of record for much of north central and northwestern Indiana. The job at the newspaper returned me to my journalism roots but also gave me access to start work on a master's degree at the University of Notre Dame and an opportunity to get the experience in television I needed to pursue a TV career. And it was a terrific place to get broadcast experience, since at that time Notre Dame owned the NBC affiliate in South Bend, and the station was right on campus. Instead of studying at a campus facility, we got to work at a commercial studio. So I worked my college classes around my work schedule at the *Trib*.

While I was working at the newspaper, I also got to pursue my passion for sports. As anyone in journalism knows, sports departments are historically under-staffed. So I would volunteer on Friday nights to cover high school basketball and football for the *Tribune*'s sports section. The guys in the sports department were more than willing to give me a chance, and were thankful for the help. As terrific as that opportunity was, that also was my first rude awakening to the reality of women covering sports.

When I went to high school football games, I usually would be able to find a corner of the press box where I could sit and watch the game. But one Friday night at South Bend Clay High School, when I made my way up to the football press box, I was turned away. "Nope, no room up here," the P.A. announcer said, even though there was at least four spaces open to his right.

I tried not to notice the slight smile he gave one of his buddies as I thanked him, walked down the bleachers, and stood by the fence that separated the stands from the field. And that's where I covered the game. I got the job done and the story filed, but I'll never forget that night. Since then, I've talked to many women who also say they've been kicked out of press boxes, so at least I know I wasn't the only one. And I've been nudged out of press rows since then. But on that night, it didn't make me feel any better to know that not everyone had my parents' opinion that I could do whatever I wanted.

Eventually I got my master's in communication arts from the University of Notre Dame and landed my first television job at WSJV-TV, then the ABC affiliate for the South Bend-Elkhart market. And even that job search had its own twists and turns. As I got closer to graduation and started looking for a job in television news, I thought I would have it made: A print reporter looking to switch to television? What news director wouldn't want to hire me with that kind of experience?

Well, as it turned out, many. Because it didn't matter what kind of journalist you were (journalist with a capital 'J' as we liked to call ourselves), news directors wanted television experience, not newspaper. So I went through months of interviews in area television markets before I got a call from a news director in Fort Wayne. Could I send an updated resume tape?

Of course. Now I just needed to get another tape together. I had just made one at the station on campus, so I couldn't impose on them to make another one. So out of the blue I called the news director for WSJV, introduced myself (he was a Ball State alum so I used that as my "in") and asked if I could come over and do a quick anchor desk read for a resume tape.

He agreed. So a couple of days later I came in during their afternoon down time, read a few stories at the desk, then did a pretend standup close for a reporter package. When I was finished, the news director, Phil Lengyel, called me into his office.

"Do you have a reason that you want to go to Fort Wayne to work?" he asked.

"No," I said. "It's just a lead I have on a reporter's job."

"Well," he continued, "we might have something coming up here soon, so let me keep you posted on our openings here."

Sure enough, a couple of weeks later there was an opening. Phil called me, and I started on the Monday after my Thursday graduation from Notre Dame. I had made it into television—even using, with some reluctance, my real name.

You see, Betsy Ross is, indeed, my God-given, Mom-given name. Not Elizabeth, not Beth, it's Betsy. And it's not like there was some premeditated scheme to give me this name—as I always say, if my parents wanted a daughter named Betsy, they would have given that name to my older sister, Jeanne. In fact, the nurse supposedly told my mother after three days of my being in the hospital without a name, "You can't call her 'Hey, You' all her life." So Betsy came from somewhere, and my middle name, Melina, came from a baby book (pronounced like Melinda without the "d," not the Greek pronunciation of Me-lee-na).

I have heard just about every comment anyone can make about my name, most of them lame, some of them cruel, but every once in a while, one that is clever. I was at the ticket window at Comerica

Park in Detroit when the woman at the counter saw my name on the credit card and said, "Your parents must have had big plans for you." I like that comment—it's probably my favorite.

As I was changing professions, I thought this was the perfect opportunity to change my name, just like all hotshot news anchors did—so I thought. I lobbied Phil to let me change my name. To Jennifer Edwards. I don't know why. I thought it was a cool name, very un-ethnic, again, just like all the other big anchors.

"Are you crazy?" he said. "You've got a name that people won't forget. You gotta keep it." And so I did. And Phil, you were right. Even though I have to endure countless bad jokes, it is memorable. Thanks.

From WSJV-TV, I headed home to the Cincinnati area and WCPO-TV, then moved up the interstate to WTHR in Indianapolis, got my first full-time sports anchoring position at SportsChannel America in New York, then headed back to Cincinnati at WLWT-TV. And while each television job (except for SportsChannel America) was as a news anchor, I used the same method I used at the *Tribune* to keep my hand in sports—I'd volunteer to help out the sports department. That was how I was able to put a sports resume reel together for SportsChannel America, and eventually how I was able to catch the attention of ESPN.

Because I was working for the NBC affiliate in Cincinnati, and because NBC had the rights to the 1996 Olympics in Atlanta, our station was really promoting the upcoming Summer Games. And, as fate would have it, we had an unusual number of area athletes involved in the Olympic trials, and eventually, the Games. Two members of the gold medal-winning "Magnificent Seven" women's gymnastics team were from Cincinnati, as was one of the coaches. Swimmers, divers, runners, shooters, rowers, you name the sport, we had an athlete competing for a spot at the Olympics. So I lobbied hard to cover their stories. That led to an opportunity to work for NBC NewsChannel, the news feed that goes to affiliate stations, on Olympic coverage. And, eventually, I got to go with our sports crew to Atlanta to cover the Olympics themselves.

At the same time ESPN was getting ready to launch ESPNews, a twenty-four-hour news channel specifically for highlights and scores. They were looking for someone who knew sports and who could anchor in half-hour blocks. Considering that most sports anchors were on the air for only about three to four minutes for their nightly sports reports, having someone who was used to anchoring for longer periods of time, and who also had sports knowledge, would be a perfect fit.

So my agent started making calls and sending my Olympics tapes to Bristol, Connecticut, and after the Games I headed to the Worldwide Leader for an interview. Now, this wasn't the first time I'd been to ESPN headquarters. When I was working at SportsChannel America, ESPN was getting ready to launch ESPN2, and I interviewed back in 1990 for a position on the new network. So I was familiar with the routine—meet everyone, sit down with a producer in the afternoon, write copy, then go on the set and anchor highlights.

Except the circumstances were very different on this interview for ESPNews. As schedules would have it, I was there on the day of the funeral for ESPN anchor Tom Mees. He was one of the first anchors for ESPN when it signed on the air in 1979 and was still with the network when he drowned in a neighbor's pool in nearby Southington, Connecticut. The shock was still apparent on everyone's face, and while I didn't have the chance to meet him, I heard wonderful stories about Tom on that day, and during the years I worked at ESPN.

Still, we all went through the motions, everyone was very nice, I did my anchor test, then couldn't wait to get on the airplane back to Cincinnati. Whether it was the pall that hung over the newsroom that day, or whether it was the mess of the construction for the new ESPNews studio, I didn't have a good feeling about the place. You know when you go into a job interview, you know in the first few minutes whether you think you'd fit in? I didn't think I'd fit in. I knew I didn't want to work there.

Of course, I was offered the job. I was to be one of the first wave of ESPNews anchors, being hired from across the country, to launch the new network.

And I said no.

I had no desire to move to Connecticut, my family and friends were all in the Midwest, and I just couldn't shake the unsettled feeling I had on that day of my interview. So I did the unthinkable—I said no to ESPN.

Until six months later, when I said yes.

What changed? Well, in television, as in any business, when bosses change, they bring in their own managers and their own style. Our station, WLWT, was first rumored to be in line to be purchased by the network itself, which was another reason I didn't want to leave for ESPN. The opportunity to work for an O & O (network owned and operated) station was tempting. But when that fell through and another purchaser took over, the new news director who came in had a "if it bleeds it leads" philosophy that didn't necessarily fit what I felt comfortable doing.

So I called my agent. "Think ESPN might still be interested?" I asked.

They were. So in April of 1997, six months after the launch of ESPN2, I was anchoring on ESPNews. I got a quick education in hockey, in soccer, in a lot of sports other than the football, basketball, baseball, and golf I was used to covering. And as much as I thought I knew about sports, my knowledge paled in comparison to most of the folks around me. For a sports fan, it was heaven.

But for all the extra folks brought into ESPN to launch ESPNews, there were still only five females of the nearly sixty anchors for all the networks: Robin Roberts, Linda Cohn, Chris McKendry, Pam Ward, and me. I still have a signed ESPN banner that I keep in my office with all five of our signatures on it. We weren't numerous, but we were proud of what we did.

For someone who was plopped down in New England with no friends and family in the area, ESPN was, and is, a terrific place to work. ESPN not only hires people who are good at their jobs, but are good people. If you weren't nice, if you weren't cordial, if you weren't respectful to your coworkers, you didn't stay. I got so used to guys holding doors open for me that it was a shock when I went to the mall and the same thing didn't happen there.

And it was a place where my writing skills were valued. It remains the only newsroom where I have worked that I wrote every word that I read. It may be more time-consuming, but that's the only way the anchors can put their own personalities into the writing. It would be silly, let's face it, for me to read something that Stuart Scott writes, and vice versa. So I loved the opportunity to put my own style into my anchoring, something that, of course, is forbidden in straight news.

In fact, one of the best compliments I received in Bristol was from a producer who said after a show, "I can't believe you ever anchored news." That's when I felt I finally arrived.

I'm often asked who were some of my more memorable interviews during my time there. One was Pedro Martinez when he was still with Montreal and had just won the Cy Young award. Despite his success, he knew he had become too pricey for the Expos to keep him, and he knew he would be leaving Montreal—but he didn't know where. He was thrilled for the honor, but very apprehensive about his future and unsure what would happen next.

Another one I remember was a satellite interview with Lance Armstrong after one of his early Tour de France wins. Just a bit of background: When these athletes do satellite interviews, they sit in one studio and the production crew around them dials up different anchors in different cities. But the satellite feed usually stays live, while the new anchor is being dialed up for the next interview.

So, the Lance Armstrong feed comes up, he's live on our monitors as he's getting ready to do our interview. In the background I hear one of the producers say, "Next interview is with ESPN and Betsy Ross."

"Betsy Ross," Lance says. And I'm thinking, oh boy, here it comes, some lame comment about my name. "Made the flag, right?" he added. And then, to no one in particular, said, "Boy, there is nothing like riding those final miles at the Tour, and everyone has their American flags out, and they're waving them as you go by. Just seeing those flags makes you so proud to be an American and know that those people support you. That's the prettiest sight around, to see that flag."

I immediately became a Lance Armstrong fan.

One interview we did on set for ESPNews almost didn't happen. It was when former Reds reliever and "Nasty Boy" Rob Dibble had just started with ESPN, and he, on occasion, would come on ESPNews to talk baseball. Now, at the Worldwide Leader, the analysts, especially ex-players and coaches, often would cut their teeth on ESPNews and then when they got good, they'd move over to ESPN.

Rob had done his time on the News side and now was working for *Baseball Tonight*, but we had some extra time on ESPNews and asked the *Baseball Tonight* producer if Rob could come on the set and give us a baseball preview.

"No, he doesn't have time," the producer said, blowing us off. "He can't do it, I won't even ask him."

Well, okay, we thought, we'll find something to fill the time.

About an hour later, Rob came over to our desks. "So what time do you want me on your show?" he asked the producer and me.

We thought you didn't have time to do an interview, we explained.

"Nope, you guys gave me my start here at ESPN before they'd take me on *Baseball Tonight*, so I'll always make time for you. Now, when do you want me in the studio?"

And I immediately became a Rob Dibble fan.

Speaking of fans, there's always a bit of the starstruck factor around ESPN, mainly because of those famous "This is SportsCenter" promotions that are shot on the ESPN campus three or four times a year. It wasn't unusual, when the production crew was on campus, to run into Pete Sampras in the cafeteria or Tiger Woods' former caddy, Fluff, in the stairwell (I've done both). Or, to find yourself in a Bon Jovi video when the band was set up in the newsroom, shooting an "It's My Life" video for the SportsCenter promos. I didn't know the words to the song when we started. But after six hours of shooting, I knew it backward and forward.

But my closest brush with fame came when I was working the early morning shift to do SportsCenter updates on the 2002 Summer Olympics in Sydney. My day started around three but ended around ten. So when the shift was done this particular day, I headed to the cafeteria to get a cup of coffee. I walked in to see that tables and chairs had been moved to make way for a billiards table, and who would be standing next to it but Jeanette Lee, the "Black Widow."

A bit of history here: If you are one of these people who watches any ESPN network any hour of the day, you're familiar with Jeanette Lee, who became a billiards star on ESPN2 when the young network was filling its programming schedule with lots of made-for-television events, like billiards competitions (usually aired between 1 a.m. and 4 a.m.). I used to watch Jeanette Lee any chance I could, because I was fascinated with how she could run a pool table. I had just purchased her book, and it was on my desk when I saw her in the cafeteria.

Maybe I can get the book and have her sign it, I thought, so I dashed across campus, grabbed the book, and went back to the caf, only to see that they had started shooting their promo. Bummer.

A couple of hours later, the field producer for the production company came into our cubicle area (I shared space with Trey Wingo) and asked if it was OK to move some chairs around, since they were going to be shooting a spot with Trey. He happened to glance and see my Jeanette Lee book on my desk.

"Hey, do you know that she's here on campus? We just finished shooting a promo with her."

"Yes, I ran over to the cafeteria, but you guys were already shooting, so I didn't want to bother her," I said.

"No bother, but I think she might be gone now," he said. "Anyway, I'll be back in a couple of hours to set up the shoot."

No problem, I said, and went back to my computer.

Ten minutes later, the producer came back. "Hey, Betsy, I want you to meet someone."

And into my little humble cubicle walked Jeanette Lee.

"Hi, how are you?" she said, offering a handshake.

I couldn't think of a thing to say. She saw her book on my desk and autographed it, gave me her business card, even gave me a gummi bear out of her candy bag. She could not have been nicer. She, and that producer, absolutely made my day.

...

During my five years at ESPN I anchored *NBA 2night*, *NHL 2night*, weekend SportsCenters, Olympic coverage during the 2002 games and, of course, ESPNews. But my most memorable day on the desk was one that none of us will forget, September 11, 2001. I was working the morning-early afternoon shift that day, so I came in around eight in the morning. I was scheduled to fly back to Cincinnati that afternoon, so I was anxious to get the day done and get home for a long mid-week break. I was happy to see that the weather was sunny and clear in Connecticut—good flying weather.

I was in the newsroom, sitting at a desk watching *The Today Show* on our monitors, when the initial report came that a small plane had hit one of the Twin Towers at the World Trade Center on the tip of Manhattan.

While the first reports of the size of the plane varied, we still just thought of it as a tragic accident, a news story for the New York area—until the second plane hit. And then we knew it was much more than an accident.

As the minutes ticked by and we realized this was a story that would reach across all broadcast spectrums, the news editors and producers started to huddle around our desks. The reports continued—all flights grounded—as many as 10,000 body bags ordered for Lower Manhattan—the news became more dire as the morning went on.

That's when we decided that, even though it was not a sports story, ESPN needed to acknowledge that we knew what was happening and we would have updates throughout the day. I went into our ESPNews studio and, broadcasting across all the ESPN networks, including international outlets, went back to my news anchor roots and reported what was happening. I stayed on the anchor desk until four that afternoon, when the next anchor came in.

It was one of the most surreal days I've ever had in broadcasting. I remember being shaken when I had to report the death of Jackie O, being emotional when I had to report that the Major League Baseball season was being cancelled. But this was just beyond anyone's comprehension. As the morning went on, the news kept getting more grim: a third plane crashing into the Pentagon; the search for the fourth plane that eventually crashed in Somerset County, Pennsylvania. Every half hour, I'd broadcast live (since the ESPN networks were all in taped programming), updating the situation, encouraging viewers to turn to their local ABC affiliates, promising responses and statements regarding how this would affect the night's sports schedules.

Through it all, I just remember repeating one phrase during my updates: "The apparent terrorist attack on the United States." Who in the world would have thought those words would come out of any of our mouths? Eventually, of course, games were suspended as the nation, and the world, tried to come to grips with this unspeakable tragedy. And that was the day that, for once, sports took a back seat to news at ESPN.

I didn't know it at the time, but that day changed my life, as it did for so many people.

That day forced so many Americans to reassess their lives, their goals, their priorities. I was one of them. I had been at ESPN for nearly five years, had just signed a new contract, but I knew that my future wasn't in Bristol. I was commuting every week from Cincinnati to Connecticut. I was tired of flying and knew that I needed to be closer to home to take care of my mother, who then was in her early eighties. So by the spring of 2002, I decided to come home to Cincinnati. It was time.

From that decision came Game Day Communications, a sports and entertainment public relations company I started with my business partner, Jackie Reau. I still stay in sports broadcasting through freelance work, play-by-play gigs, and radio interviews.

But being at ESPN is every sports fan's dream and one of the highlights of my career. Sure, I've heard and read stories about how the atmosphere there was not necessarily friendly to females, but I personally never felt it. I felt accepted as a sports anchor and welcomed to the ESPN family. I still have close friends from my Bristol days, and I am grateful to the folks there for the opportunity to be part of the best sports operation on the planet.

I'm fortunate that I can continue to make a living in the business of sports, something that might not have been possible ten or twenty years ago. It is because of the perseverance of so many women before me, that I can be in this profession. They put up with a lot, so that I could follow my passion. We who are reaping the benefits of their hard work owe them a great deal of thanks.

chapter 2

It All Started on a Tennis Court

"My life, since I've been twelve years old, is about equal rights and opportunities for both men and women, girls and boys."

—Billie Jean King

*F*or someone whose impact on society is huge, Billie Jean King is actually quite small.

In fact, she's a five-feet-five dynamo who, at the same time, is wonderfully down to earth. That's the first thing I noticed when I had the honor of interviewing her in May of 2010, in conjunction with Major League Baseball's Civil Rights Beacon Awards. The annual event recognizes individuals whose lives are emblematic of the spirit of the Civil Rights Movement. Billie Jean King was receiving the Beacon of Change award for having an impact on society through words and actions, and I had the chance to interview her just moments before she went on the field to be honored.

Of course, her work in civil rights and equal rights has spanned her lifetime, not to mention her success on the tennis court. But for most of us, the seminal moment of Billie Jean's career was September 20, 1973, the night of the "Battle of the Sexes" match with Bobby Riggs. That evening, on prime time television, she showed that a female athlete could win under pressure, facing a self-proclaimed "male chauvinist pig" who, just weeks before, had defeated the top-ranked female player, Margaret Court, in straight sets—on Mother's Day, no less.

In her book, *Pressure Is a Privilege,* King talks about the Riggs match, which came a year after Title IX was passed, guaranteeing women and girls equal opportunities to play sports. Speaking about the match, she writes: "I wanted to make sure I understood every aspect of what I was getting myself into. I asked myself: Can I afford to lose this match? What are the consequences? The pros were simple: If I won, it might get the minds and hearts of Americans to begin to match up on issues of equality, and, I hoped, create real support for Title IX."

Even famed sportswriter Frank Deford, in his *Sports Illustrated* article "Sometimes the Bear Eats You" (March 29, 2010) mentioned the magnitude of the King-Riggs match: "I was very fortunate to be covering tennis when Billie Jean King took the bull by the horns. Billie Jean more than anyone else raised my consciousness. Here she was, virtually running a sport, getting up at 6 a.m. after a night match to appear on *Sunrise in Cincinnati* or some other TV

Billie Jean King

show, serving as a symbol for a whole movement, taking a lot of crap from people who didn't appreciate her—and winning championships.

"I *knew* she would beat Bobby Riggs in their Battle of the Sexes in '73," Deford continued. "Only two or three times in my life have I been dead sure of an outcome in sport, and that time is at the top of the list. Apart from the fact that Billie Jean was simply a better player than Bobby was then, and immune to pressure, she was really a lot like him. They both knew how to work a crowd, only Bobby was in it for the con, Billie Jean for a cause."

Frank Deford got it absolutely right. Let's face it, both Riggs and Billie Jean had an agenda. Both were promoters: Riggs promoting himself in the twilight of his career, and Billie Jean, promoting her cause of equality. The match brought the issue of women's rights into everyday conversation and advanced the cause. Would the progress of equal rights, especially in sports, grind to a halt if she had lost? Probably not, but progress may have been slowed. Good thing women didn't have to find out.

That game, however, is just one event in Billie Jean King's legacy of fighting for equal rights. She founded the Women's Tennis Association, Women's Sports Foundation, *Women's Sports* magazine, and co-founded World TeamTennis. She won thirty-nine Grand Slam singles, doubles, and mixed doubles tennis titles, including a record twenty titles at Wimbledon.

She continues to be a champion of social change and equality, and her awards and honors are many: Received the Presidential Medal of Freedom; named one of the "100 Most Important Americans of the 20th Century" by *Life* magazine; named Global Mentor for Gender Equality by the United Nations Educational, Scientific and Cultural Organization (UNESCO); received the NCAA President's Gerald R. Ford Award in 2009, recognizing her contributions to improving higher education and intercollegiate athletics; and perhaps the most meaningful honor, in 2006, when the National Tennis Center, home of the U. S. Open, was renamed the USTA Billie Jean King National Tennis Center in honor of King's contributions to tennis, sports, and society both on and off the court.

She has carried the cause of equal rights for decades, and because of her efforts, she received the Beacon Award from Major League Baseball in 2010, along with baseball Hall of Famer Willie Mays and entertainer Harry Belafonte. Before the on-field ceremonies, I had the opportunity to interview her for Fox 19 Sports in Cincinnati. We talked about her work, her legacy, and her future, and I started by asking her about the Beacon Award from MLB:

"What it does for me is it reminds me of the responsibility I still have and also, it keeps that fire in the belly going, to focus on it and to thank the people before me and try to get the younger ones to carry the baton. I think those are the important things to do to keep all the generations working together, being very thankful for the people who sacrificed for us, before us, and for us to keep working.

"My life, since I've been twelve years old, is about equal rights and opportunities for both men and women, girls and boys. And I still have the same exact fire at sixty-six. So I'm going to keep going until my last breath, if I can help in any way to make a difference.

"I knew at twelve years old, when I had this epiphany about wanting to make a difference for equal rights and opportunities. I knew if I didn't become number one, particularly as a woman, as a girl, that no one would ever listen to me. So that was a driving force to be number one, because it created an opportunity for me to be able to speak out and people might listen.

"It's much harder for women, though. People don't tend to listen to us as much as men. There are a lot of assumptions, so I knew I had to be at least number one, and then also, I knew that we had to make tennis professional. I even knew, at twelve years old, I wanted to be in a professional sport, and I really wanted to be in a team sport, which is what I do now.

"I'm a small-business woman. I have been since 1968, which most people don't realize. I've either owned tournaments, and now I own the majority of the World TeamTennis league, and our league has men and women with equal contribution to the team effort, on a level playing field. So if you ever see a World TeamTennis match, you see my philosophy on life."

On the "Battle of the Sexes" matchup with Bobby Riggs: "I actually realized the magnitude of the event when I said yes to him, for two months before we played. So I understood it was about history, it was about men and women, their own emotions about themselves, about the opposite gender. Title IX had just been passed, June 23, 1972, and I played Bobby in '73, and I really wanted to win that match to change people's hearts and minds to actually match the legislation of Title IX."

On advice she gives to young people, especially young women: "I want young people to know history. Because the more you know about history, the more you know about yourself, and how you fit into this universe. And then from having that knowledge, it will help you and direct you to know where you can make a difference in this world. And also know your strengths and weaknesses.

"So you must have self-awareness, but you must understand history if you want to be leader. If you want to make a difference, it really helps to understand history and then how you're going to shape the future. When I talk to the young tennis players on the WTA Tour, I say, 'You have to shape the future for the next five to ten years. How do you want to do that?'

"And they're stunned, because they've never thought of themselves shaping anything. But they are shaping the future. Every generation shapes the next five to ten years, twenty years. So it's very important to kind of wake up young people to start thinking about their legacy."

Then when the interview was over and I was shaking hands to thank her for her time, she said to me, "And how about you, are they treating you well here?" In all my years of covering sports, I'd never been asked that. So I gave her a quick synopsis of my sports work, my experience in the market, and said, yes, I'd worked with many of these people for some twenty years, and they do treat me well, thanks to the work that Billie Jean and many other women had done.

"So pay it forward," she said. "Make sure that the next generation has those opportunities as well."

It's a responsibility that Billie Jean, and all the women featured in this book, take seriously. Here are some of the women, especially in sports media, who have paid it forward to allow this generation to pursue their dreams of working in sports:

Sadie Kneller Miller

While Midy Morgan is considered the first female sportswriter for her coverage of horse racing (and livestock news—let's hope the subjects were not related) for the *New York Times* in 1869, women in media have Sadie Kneller Miller to thank for giving them a regular sports beat. Sadie graduated from Western Maryland College in 1885 with a penchant for journalism, and caught on with the *Westminster Democratic Advocate*. Later, she moved to Baltimore with her parents and began writing for the *Baltimore Telegram*.

Her work at the *Telegram* included covering the Baltimore Orioles, and she became known as "the only woman baseball reporter in the country." Her interest in writing led her to take up photography, and she translated that skill to some landmark assignments, including a notable one with *Leslie's Illustrated Weekly*. She turned in photos of Spanish-American War activities at the Naval Academy in Annapolis, and they were so good she got a permanent position at *Leslie's*.

She stayed there for sixteen years, and during that time had such assignments as the Baltimore fire of 1904, the Taft inauguration, five Democratic conventions, and portraits of Teddy Roosevelt and Susan B. Anthony, the last formal photo taken of the suffragist.

She may have been a pioneer in sports, but she also broke down barriers in overseas reporting. She became known as the only female war correspondent in the world when she covered fighting in Morocco; she described the gold rush in the Yukon; she did interviews from Cuba to leper colonies and Czarist Russia, and interviewed Pancho Villa at his base in the Mexican mountains.

The ironic thing about Sadie's sports coverage—many readers probably didn't even know they were reading the work of a female sportswriter. Her stories carried the byline "SKM," probably to hide her gender.

Women who covered sports in the 1920s include Mary Bostwick, covering the Indianapolis Motor Speedway for the *Indianapolis Star;* Dorothy Bough, sportswriter for the *Philadelphia Inquirer;* Nettie George Speedy, sports reporter for the *Chicago Defender;* Nan O'Reilly, golf editor of the *New York Evening News;* Cecile Ladu, sports editor of the *Albany Times Union.*

Lorena Hickok

Lorena might be best known as one of Eleanor Roosevelt's closest friends, but she first was a journalist. Growing up in Wisconsin, she entered Lawrence College in Appleton in 1912 but left after a year to take a job with the *Battle Creek Evening News* for seven dollars a week.

She eventually got a job at the *Milwaukee Sentinel* as a society editor, later went to the *Minneapolis Tribune,* then went to New York to try to get a job covering World War I. When that didn't work out, she returned to the *Tribune* and eventually was assigned to cover the University of Minnesota football team during the glory days of Big Ten football. Here's a sample from the 1924 game between Minnesota and the University of Illinois and its star running back, Red Grange: "Again and again, 'Red' Grange hugged the ball to his ribs and started one of his famous runs," she wrote. "Again and again he started and dropped, with three or four Gophers on top of him."

She eventually joined the Associated Press to write features for the national wire service, covering politics and major stories such as the Lindbergh kidnapping. But her assignment with the University of Minnesota made her the first female beat writer to cover a men's sports team.

Margaret Goss

Although she wrote the column for only a year and a half, Margaret Goss was able to make history during her time as a columnist for the *New York Herald Tribune*. In 1924 and '25, Goss described herself as the first American female journalist to cover women's sports for a daily newspaper, and also was the first woman with a regular, bylined sports column.

That column, "Women in Sport," gave Goss an opportunity to talk about women athletes and their accomplishments at a time when they were just making strides in the world of sports. Goss's timing was perfect, as the 1920s often are described as the "Golden Age" of sports journalism, spawning such legendary sportswriters as Grantland Rice (whose column often shared space with Goss).

Mary Garber

When the sports editor at the *Twin City Sentinel* in Winston-Salem, North Carolina, went off to war during World War II, another staffer (and sports fan), Mary Garber, took his place. When he returned, he got his old job back, and Mary moved back to her pre-war assignment on the paper's society pages. It didn't take long for the editors to figure out Mary knew more about sports than society, so she returned to the sports pages, where she stayed for four decades.

If these earlier women sportswriters were pioneers, then Mary is the godmother. Mary Ellen Garber was born in New York in 1916. Her father was a contractor who moved the family to Winston-Salem in the 1920s. Mary graduated from Hollins College in 1938 and eventually found her way to the newspaper and sportswriting.

Though in her early days she mainly covered high school sports in the area, she went on to assignments involving all types of sports, including football, basketball, baseball, track, tennis, softball, you name it, at all levels from rec leagues to college. She also covered minor league baseball, international track and field, and Davis Cup tennis.

Perhaps more groundbreaking, she reported on black high schools and the historically black colleges in the area—schools that often were ignored by the daily newspapers—during the segregation years of the 1950s and 1960s.

"Nobody cared much about black players forty years ago," Clarence "Big House" Gaines, the Hall of Fame basketball coach at Winston-Salem State University told *Sports Illustrated* in 2000. "But Miss Mary covered a lot of things that weren't too popular. She went out of her way to see that everybody got a fair shake."

To Miss Mary, it was all just part of the job. "When I started working in sports full time, it seemed to me that black parents were as interested in what their kids were doing as white parents were," she said in a 1990 interview.

She also had to fight for equal access to do her job, especially since in the early years she was barred from locker rooms and press boxes because she was a woman. In 1946, even though she had the right credentials, she had to cover a Duke football game while she was sitting in the stands with the coaches' wives.

Her managing editor protested the move and told the Athletic Coast Conference athletic directors to get used to it—the paper wouldn't cover their games with any other reporter but Miss Mary. They relented and let her in the press box, but the ACC Sportswriters Association and Football Writers Association denied her membership for many years. When she eventually was granted membership, she ended up as the association's president and served on its board of directors.

She worked as a full-time sportswriter at the *Sentinel* and *Winston-Salem Journal* until 1986, when she retired at age seventy. She then worked part-time until 2002. Along the way she picked up numerous awards, including sports journalism's highest honor, the Red Smith Award, given annually by the Associated Press for major contributions to sports journalism.

Other honors include election to the North Carolina Sports Hall of Fame in 1996, and induction into the National Sportscasters and Sportswriters Association and Hall of Fame. The Association of Women in Sports Media (AWSM) renamed its annual pioneer award in her honor in 2006.

Mary Garber died in 2008 in a retirement home in Winston-Salem at the age of ninety-two, but she lived long enough to see a generation of women follow her footsteps in the field of sports reporting. Her quote as she received the Red Smith Award reflects her legacy: "I hope I have helped. I hope some little girl out there knows now that she can be a sportswriter if she wants to be." In fact, the first winner of the AWSM Pioneer Award was Lesley Visser, the NFL's first female beat writer.

Representative Patsy Takemoto Mink

Say what you will about the administration of Richard Nixon, but one of the landmark pieces of legislation that came out of that tumultuous time was the Educational Amendment to the Civil Rights Act of 1964, known as Title IX. The amendment, prohibiting gender discrimination by federally funded institutions, was written by Representative Patsy Mink of Hawaii, mainly from an outgrowth of the adversities Mink faced through college. In fact, the amendment itself was renamed in 2002 the Patsy T. Mink Equal Opportunity in Education Act.

The amendment itself hardly sounds controversial: "No person in the United States shall, on the basis of sex, be excluded from participation in, or denied the benefits of, or be subjected to discrimination under any educational program or activity receiving federal assistance." But what was supposed to jump-start women's participation in sports has often turned into a battle of the sexes for athletic access.

This isn't intended to be an argument of the pros and cons of Title IX. What is clear, though, is that the amendment has opened doors for many young girls and women who might otherwise not have had the opportunity to participate in organized sports.

...

The following women contributed some early "firsts" for women in sports.

- Jane Gross, when at *Newsday*, was the first woman reporter in an NBA locker room.

- Betty Cuniberti, *San Francisco Chronicle*, covered the Oakland Raiders and became the first woman to cover an NFL team from training camp through the Super Bowl. In 1981 at the *Washington Star* she became the first woman to receive the National Headliner Award for Consistently Outstanding Sports Writing.

- Lesley Visser, *Boston Globe*, covered the New England Patriots.

- Melissa Ludke of *Sports Illustrated* was famously barred from interviewing players in the clubhouse during the World Series. *SI*'s publisher, Time, Inc., filed suit, and the next year a federal court judge ruled that male and female reporters should have equal access to locker rooms.

- Michele Himmelberg at the *Fort Myers News-Press* needed her newspaper to threaten a lawsuit against the Tampa Bay Buccaneers to win equal access for her to the team's locker room. Two years later, Himmelberg was at the *Sacramento Bee* where a lawsuit was filed to let her into the 49ers' locker room.

- Gayle Gardner was the first full-time female sports anchor at a major network (NBC).

- Jane Chastain (my personal role model, by the way) was the first female sports reporter to regularly cover the MLB and NFL and who, eventually, moved to CBS Sports.

- Yankees broadcaster Suzyn Waldman was the first woman to provide color commentary for a nationally broadcast MLB game.

- Robin Roberts was the first woman to serve as host for the legendary *Wide World of Sports* series on ABC.

- Pam Ward was the first woman to serve as play-by-play announcer for ESPN college football.

- Sally Jenkins was the first woman to win the Associated Press Sports Editors' top columnist award in the largest circulation category.

- Helene Elliott of the *Los Angeles Times* was the first woman inducted into the Hockey Hall of Fame.

And that's just in the field of sports journalism. Others have paved the way for women in the management and administrative areas in sports, including:

- Val Ackerman, the first president of the Women's National Basketball Association and the first woman selected to direct USA Basketball;

- Elaine Weddington, the first woman and second African-American to serve in upper management in Major League Baseball (Boston Red Sox);

- Violet Palmer and Dee Kantner, the first female referees in the NBA;

- Sarah Thomas, first woman to referee a college football bowl game.

Those are just a fraction of the women recording "firsts" in the field of sports, and continue to do so every day in media, management, coaching, and playing.

chapter 3

From Radio to TV,
Women Change Sportscasting

*"Some women love sports and get into television. Others love
television and get into sports."*

—Lesley Visser, CBS Sports

*H*ey, Liguori, what's the story?"

During my time at SportsChannel America on Long Island, my
entertainment in my studio apartment in Long Beach was the radio
that was always tuned to the legendary sports talk radio station
WFAN-AM. And very early on weekend mornings, I would often
wake up to that catch phrase from Ann Liguori's radio show.

If you've listened to sports talk radio in the East for any amount of time, you've heard that phrase, as Ann Liguori brought interviews with sports headliners to WFAN, the first all-sports radio station in the country. In the macho world of sports talk radio, Ann Liguori was one of the station's original show hosts. In fact, WFAN was a bit of a trailblazer of its own when it came to women in sports—besides having Ann as a talk show host, the first voice

Ann Liguori

ever heard on the station was that of another female sportscaster, Suzyn Waldman, the Yankees' color analyst, who christened the station with a sports update.

If you haven't heard her sports updates for Westwood One or WFAN, then you may have seen her syndicated show, *Sports Innerview with Ann Liguori* or read her book, *A Passion for Golf, Celebrity Musings About the Game*. She's interviewed sports legends and business leaders, entertainers and musicians, while telling their stories about the games they love. I've watched her interviews, especially those with professional golfers, for years, and I've always admired her style. Ann has a relaxed manner with the knack to ask just the right questions.

For Ann, the journey to WFAN and beyond started in Cincinnati, where she was born. Then her family moved to a Cleveland suburb,

Brecksville, where she fell in love with sports. "Every day after school, all the guys would come to our house," she said. "We had a big back yard, and we'd play sports. And I was the first one picked on a lot of the teams. Back then I could run faster than a lot of the guys, and I was always very athletic. I earned sixteen letters—four varsity letters a year, every year, in high school."

Between the games in the back yard and the teams in high school, though, Ann had a tough time finding a place to play. "One of the most devastating memories to me was when I finally got into junior high, in eighth grade, there literally were no sports teams for girls. I just could not believe how disappointing and devastating it was for me at that point, because I was so athletic in elementary school. There was really nothing for girls except for cheerleading.

"So my dad and I put a track team together from our school that competed in the AAU in track meets throughout northeastern Ohio, and so I found an outlet where I could at least compete in track and field. And then, thank goodness, when Title IX was passed, there were opportunities, and by the time I was a freshman in high school, there were sports teams for girls that we could compete in."

Ann's passion for sports and her interest in broadcasting led her to the University of South Florida, where she was able to watch then-sports reporter and anchor Gayle Sierens on Tampa's NBC affiliate. "Gayle was a tremendous role model for me at the time because as I was going to USF and living in Tampa, I could see a woman actually anchoring sports on television. Gayle went on to become the first woman on network television on NBC Sports to work as a color analyst for an NFL game."

And another educational opportunity led her to New York. "I earned a fellowship through the International Radio and TV Society that brought me right up to Manhattan out of college. They picked about twenty-five graduates to come to New York City in a fellowship program where they paid all our expenses for six weeks, put us up in the dorms at New York University, and we learned all about the business. And it wasn't just about the on-air side of the business. We learned about marketing and sales and production, and we had the opportunity to really network with some of the heavyweights in the business.

"One of our informational seminars was at CBS Sports. And I can remember walking in there and sitting down in the conference room and being so fascinated with the sports the network was covering and how they went about it. And I knew that the second I walked in there that sports broadcasting was for me, particularly with my athletic background and passion for a variety of sports. So I started my career in an unusual way. I went to New York City directly out of college and stayed. The Big Apple—the media capital in the world! That's one heck of a place to pursue an on-air career in sports broadcasting. And as it turned out, I was eventually able to combine all my loves— hosting, interviewing, reporting, producing, writing, running a business, creating, marketing, selling, and distributing shows."

Ann's career started with freelancing gigs in sports, mainly as a producer at the ABC Radio Network. Her opportunity to switch from producer to reporter came courtesy of the 1984 Olympics in Los Angeles. "They needed a tennis correspondent—it was a demonstration sport at the time—I knew tennis, and they needed somebody to go and cover tennis, so I raised my hand and they sent me, and that was how I got my big break."

And that, as so often happens, led to another big break that landed her as the first woman to host a sports show on the first sports talk radio station. "The people who put WFAN together had heard me on the ABC Radio Network, and they had seen my byline in the sports pages of *USA Today*. WFAN wanted a woman to host a show. It's funny. I learned that I was hired to host my own show on WFAN Radio by reading about it in the newspaper! They hadn't even told me officially yet, but I read it in one of the radio-TV columns.

"Those were interesting days because if I had a penny for everybody who said, 'All-sports radio? That's never going to work,' I'd probably be a lot wealthier today. I knew back then that the station would become a success story because of all the professional and college sports teams in the New York metropolitan area. With the Yankees, the Mets, the Giants, Jets, Knicks, New Jersey Nets, and three professional hockey teams in the area, there is a lot to talk about on an all-sports radio station! And the New York audiences are some of the most passionate sports fans in the country."

So in 1987, sports-talk WFAN signed on with, not just Ann Liguori, but with sports broadcasting names such as Jim Lampley, Howie Rose, Greg Gumbel, and Steve Somers. As with a lot of new ventures, though, there were some growing pains at WFAN. "After the first year and a half, they realized that they spent way too much money and hired way too many people. So they ended up firing most of their staff, including all the women. Somehow I managed to hang on there with a weekly show for twenty-two straight years and still going." Instead of being a full-time employee, Ann became a contributor to the station.

And that led Ann to her second career, as the host of the syndicated *Sports Innerview with Ann Liguori* show, and the decision to be her own producer—essentially, to own her own show. "I always wanted to interview different personalities in sports and entertainment and business, and so I thought, well, if I'm going to do that, I think I'm going to have to do it myself. Because back then, and even today, the programmers and TV executives really were not hiring women to host their own sports talk shows. You'd think it'd be different today, but it really isn't." Before Oprah, it was rare for a woman to produce her own broadcast content.

Some encouragement from a program executive at MSG Network helped Ann figure out how to do that. "She said, 'Ann, if you would like to have a show on the network, we will air it. But you're going to have to put it together yourself (meaning, acquiring your own sponsors to pay for it!). Well, that was a good enough 'window' for me at the time. I thought, if I can get this show put together, financially, MSG Network will air the show, and then I could start distributing the show to other networks. I knew I would have to get the sponsorship dollars to basically produce a show, and that is probably the most difficult part of the process.

"Having covered all these sporting events throughout my career, writing for USA Today and working for ABC Radio Network, I had met so many different people, not only athletes but also corporate sponsors. So I knew that I could go back to some of these corporate people that I had met and at least get a meeting with some of them to see if they'd be willing to come in and sponsor my interview series.

"So that's basically what I did. I set up all these meetings, and one of my very first meetings was with Volvo and their CEO at the time, Bjorn Ahlstrom. I'll never forget going to his office in New Jersey, in the Volvo North America headquarters, and having about ten minutes to pitch my idea. Lucky for me, he and his wife were huge tennis fans—after all, they were sponsoring the tennis circuit back then—and I was able to talk him into sponsoring the first thirteen of my shows.

"Of course I told him that I would get [John] McEnroe and Martina [Navratilova] and [Jimmy] Connors and Chrissy [Evert] and all the top tennis players to agree to be my guests on the show. At the time I didn't know how I was going to do it, but I knew I'd have to come through because I promised I would get them. This man literally gave me the opportunity of a lifetime, and not only did he say 'yes' to sponsoring the show, he also agreed to pay my production company up front which is unheard of in the advertising world.

"So with my first sponsor on board, I was able to land Sharp Electronics, who came in for eight straight years as my main sponsor, which is quite a track record for any one company to sponsor one series. And I have Loretta Volpe to thank for that, a dynamo in the advertising business who has been very supportive of me and a mentor to many women and men in the business through the years. And since then, I've worked with dozens of sponsors, which kept *Sports Innerview with Ann Liguori* on the air on cable sports networks throughout the country, each week, from 1989 to 2003. What a run! And obviously selling sponsorships is not the easiest task, as for every company that said 'yes,' there were, say, twenty-five companies that turned it down. It was a result of much determination, hard work, and persistence."

So *Sports Innerview with Ann Liguori* was launched, and it launched with one of the biggest legends in sports: Mickey Mantle.

"Mickey was the toast of the town, had his own restaurant, Mickey Mantle's on Central Park South in Manhattan, and he granted me the interview. I went to his restaurant to tape the interview. He was the most charming, riveting storyteller I'd ever heard. And it was also special because it was my very first show, and I was debuting with a huge star, 'The Mick,' and he just made it so easy for me and just so interesting.

"The interview was also moving as Mickey cried when he was talking about losing his son to Hodgkin's Disease. He also got emotional talking about the late Roger Maris, because so many people thought he and Roger disliked each other immensely as they were competing for the home run record. Quite the contrary, he and Roger were very good friends. There was actually a ball encased in the wall by his favorite booth in the restaurant, and during the interview, Mickey took the ball out of its encasement and he said, 'Ann, look at this signature from Roger,' and it said, 'To Mick, my best friend, love, Rog.' He was just very sentimental during that interview."

Another of Ann's favorite interviews was with another baseball legend, Ted Williams. "When Ted came back to Boston for the [MLB] All-Star Game in 1999, he was ailing. But his son, John Henry, said, 'My dad is not well, but if you come here at about eleven o'clock, he will have just gotten up from his nap, and it should be a really good time for you to talk to him.'

"And for forty minutes, I enjoyed a fascinating discussion with Ted Williams, who was a baseball genius and so charming as well. And he came back to Boston obviously much older and much softer, with a whole different appreciation for the fans there. And he apologized for anything he ever did in his career that turned off the fans in Boston. It was just a special interview for me because Ted did not do a lot of them, and he really opened up and shared a lot with me. And it was the first time he and John Henry were ever interviewed on television together. I did the third segment interviewing the both of them."

So, yes, she interviewed the Mick and the Splinter and, as promised, Martina and Chrissy, along with Yogi Berra, Alice Cooper, Kevin Costner, Jim Brown, Wilt Chamberlain, Brett Favre, Tim Tebow, Billie Jean King, Greg Norman, and hundreds of others for her syndicated show and her radio segments. She's traveled the world covering golf, tennis, and the Olympics. She has her own sketch of Snoopy on the golf course putting, drawn by Peanuts creator Charles Schulz during their interview. Her foundation, the Ann Liguori Foundation, organizes an annual charity golf tournament and dinner dance in the Hamptons in New York to raise money for cancer prevention, research, and care. Each year the foundation donates to the American Cancer Society and to dozens of other charities and organizations that work in this field. In addition, the foundation provides a scholarship in her late brother Jim's name to mass communications students at the University of South Florida in Tampa, where Ann, Jim, her sister Jean, and brother Dan all went to college. The scholarship is in memory of Jim, who died of leukemia when he was twenty-two-years-old. Ann's father, Frank Liguori, died of cancer a year and a half earlier.

Her love of sports and her drive to follow that passion has led her to a life she says she hopes will have a positive influence on people. Ann offers this advice to other women: "Dream big. Work hard. Stay focused. Have faith. Set your goals and then work harder than the next person to achieve them. Don't be discouraged by setbacks. Learn from them and keep going. And have a passion for what you are doing."

...

True confession here: I watch Lesley Visser every time she's on the sidelines.

Not to critique her coverage of the NFL; I know she's got that down pat.

I watch her to see what she's wearing.

Because Lesley is out there in all kinds of weather: 90 degrees in Florida, 20 degrees in Green Bay. And every time, she is dressed for the occasion: Appropriate for the weather, appropriate for her job. Because the way reporters, especially sideline reporters, dress, I feel, reflects on their approach to their jobs. From the start, Lesley has approached her career the same way she dresses: With class. I've always thought she was the coolest thing. Still do.

Her sports resume is a long one: First woman enshrined into the Pro Football Hall of Fame in Canton; first woman assigned to work *Monday Night Football*; first woman on a Super Bowl sideline; first woman to handle the Super Bowl trophy presentation; only sportscaster, male or female, to work on the network broadcasts of the Final Four, Super Bowl, World Series, NBA Finals, Triple Crown, Olympics, U.S. Open tennis, and the World Figure Skating Championship.

She was named one of the Ten Pioneers of Women's Sports by *USA Today*, one of the Hundred Luminaries in the history of CBS, and voted the Number One Female Sportscaster of all time by members of the American Sportscasters Association. And she's not done yet. In the fall of 2009 she was the color analyst for a televised preseason NFL game between the Miami Dolphins and New Orleans Saints, the first time a female broadcaster sat in the analyst's seat.

"I've done these preseason games for the last couple of years for the local CBS affiliate," Lesley said, "and I do them with Bob Griese and Nat Moore, great former Dolphins, and Bob had a conflict so they said, 'Well, Lesley, would you like to go up in the booth?' And I have to tell you, it was the first time in years that I was really nervous.

"I knew that I knew the football, I'm very comfortable with that, but I didn't know the mechanics. There isn't a camera right in front of you, it's somewhere out there in the field, but after a few minutes it was just like, okay, this is just a game and we can talk about it. But I very much enjoyed it, and I absolutely believe, sooner than later, you will see a woman doing that."

Lesley first thought about a job in sports when she was growing up in the Cincinnati suburb of Wyoming, Ohio. "I remember, I was about ten years old, and I told my mother, I said, 'You know what? I want to be a sportswriter.' Now, the job did not exist for women. I could just as easily have said, 'I'm going to move to Mars.' But my mom, who was a high school English teacher, was so great. Instead of saying, 'Oh, girls don't do that, you can't do that,' she just looked at me and she said, 'You know, sometimes you have to cross when the sign says don't walk.' It was really profound. And so I was just determined I was going to be a sportswriter."

Lesley also played the game. In high school she captained the field hockey and basketball teams, and as a sophomore was named the school's best athlete. But in the back of her mind was her childhood goal to not only play sports, but to write about sports.

She headed to Boston College to do just that. "My sports editor at Boston College was [author and *New York Daily News* columnist] Mike Lupica. And Mike was so confident. I can remember Mike, a sophomore in college, telling Yaz [Red Sox great Carl Yastrzemski] to retire. I wrote for the Boston College paper, and then I won a Carnegie Foundation grant that was open to twenty women across the country who wanted to go into

Lesley Visser

jobs that were 90 percent male, which in 1974, those were all white-collar jobs. Women were just starting to go to law school, just starting to go to medical school. I remember a woman from Michigan got it for archeology, and I'd actually applied for sportswriting, and I won one of them. I went to work at the *Boston Globe*, which, as you know, had a brilliant sports section."

How brilliant? Well, walking into the sports department there was like walking into a sportswriting hall of fame wing.

"I was terrified. *Sports Illustrated* recently named the *Boston Globe* sports section the best of all time from 1975-1980. Our staff was Peter Gammons on baseball, Bob Ryan on basketball, Bud Collins on tennis, Will McDonough on football. Another one of our guys, John Powers, won a Pulitzer, so it was just staggeringly competitive. But it was the best of everything for me. They were pretty accepting.

"The guys at the *Globe* knew that I would work hard, they knew I had a pretty good sports background in terms of knowledge. I was one of those kids who read the *Sporting News*, had read box scores since I was eight, and I understood the magnitude of what the *Boston Globe* sports section was.

"But I would get letters in the mail, 'I don't want to read you or any other broad in the *Globe*'s sports section.' So yes, I have a lot of hard-earned scar tissue, but I loved it, I loved it. I looked at it like the challenge, and my passion, were greater than the obstacles."

Her work at the *Globe* landed her the job of covering the New England Patriots, becoming the NFL's first female beat writer, which offered her a whole new set of challenges and obstacles. "I remember grinding my teeth all the way to the Patriots practice in the car, because I just did not know how this would go. This was in 1976, I was the beat writer, I was young, and I remember the credentials, which actually said, 'No women or children in the press box.' Now, can you imagine anybody going to his or her job, and right there, in front of you, it says you are not welcome.

"But I had great support. The *Boston Globe* was so powerful, and the fact that they had assigned me, and they had spoken to the Patriots and said, 'Look, you are going to have a woman beat writer.' And you know, it went okay. It was just difficult for everyone because they hadn't known women in professional jobs.

"The coach was Chuck Fairbanks, and I remember the first time I went to interview him, I asked him something about one of his linebackers, and he said, 'You know, you ought to go to lunch with my daughter. You're about the same age.' Honestly, he didn't mean to be diminishing, but I was from another planet to those people."

So did Lesley have any second thoughts about making the move to the NFL? "No. I was so excited, I really welcomed it. You know how, when you're young, you're kind of protected by your innocence? I had some goals, and I did want eventually to cover the NFL. I wanted to cover the Final Four. I wanted to do a World Series. I'd grown up pretty hard core basketball, baseball, football, and then after that it was just a blessing. I've covered fifteen Wimbledons, which was really helpful, because when I went on to CBS, there was nothing that CBS put on that I hadn't covered."

Which brings us to her move to television, when she started with CBS Sports in 1984 and then became full time in 1987. Her co-workers—like Gammons, Collins, McDonough, even Lupica—made the transition to television, so it wasn't a foreign concept to her. However, it did require an adjustment. "It was interesting because not all people make it. You think everybody's doing it, but they are very different skills. Television is a different kind of communication. I'd never worked with a teleprompter; everything I've done has been in the field or all from my brain. What worked for me was instead of writing on deadline, I would just speak on deadline. That was very helpful to me, because I'd had to organize thoughts and sentences so often for ten years in print.

"When CBS asked me to work in the early eighties, when I started doing some features for them, honestly at first I was like, 'Why would I leave the *Globe?* This was before ESPN had taken hold, CNN was just evolving, so there were the three big networks, and back then, print was very powerful. And I really struggled. I thought TV, when I was growing up, was just for Walter Cronkite and Huntley and Brinkley, it wasn't for a kid out of Boston College. I thought long and hard about it, and then I said, 'You know, why not learn to flex a different set of muscles at a very high level.'"

Her television experience eventually led her in the late 1990s to the sideline job on ABC's *Monday Night Football*, becoming the first woman to join the storied and very popular broadcast and helping define the job, especially for women.

But remember, television is a business. And Lesley got caught in a bit of a ratings numbers game in 2000, when, after viewership for *Monday Night Football* slumped, she was replaced on the sidelines by a younger Melissa Stark. The decision didn't sit well with her colleagues. Said Tracy Dodds, then associate sports editor of the *Cleveland Plain Dealer* and former president of the Association for Women in Sports Media, "I was very upset when they let Lesley go. Here was a reporter, a journalist, who happens to be good-looking. She had top reporting skills and yet she was out."

Also commenting was Donna deVarona, who at the same time had a $50 million age- and sex-discrimination lawsuit pending against ABC. "I would have liked to have seen Lesley in the booth," she said, "but it's pretty hard to be a pioneer."

Lesley certainly wasn't the only target of former NBC Sports head Don Ohlmeyer, who was brought in before the 2000 season to revive *Monday Night Football*. Analyst Boomer Esiason, producer Ken Wolfe, and director Craig Janoff all got the boot, along with Lesley. But it didn't take long for her to land on her feet, as she returned to CBS Sports for NFL, college basketball, and U.S. Open tennis coverage.

Through it all, Lesley didn't blame the decision on her age—she was forty-six at the time. "This was not a case where you can paint the network with this [discrimination] brush," she told *USA Today's* Rudy Martzke. "This was one man's decision. I was qualified for that job. I worked the NFL beat for twenty years."

While *Monday Night Football* has gone through a series of sideline reporters since Lesley was there, her time on the show has, almost by default, made her the "dean" of female sideline reporters. So it makes sense that she would be asked for her opinion of the 2009 Erin Andrews incident, when the ESPN sideline reporter was stalked and videotaped in her hotel room by an Illinois insurance executive who received a two-and-a-half-year prison sentence for recording the videos, then posting them on the Internet.

"When it first happened, I had four hundred reporters calling me," Lesley admitted. "What I saw happening was she became a thing, or a topic, and people forgot that she was a person. And she was in tremendous pain, just tremendous pain through all this. Instead, it just became a blogger's delight. Erin had become so popular that I think she sort of morphed into this 'thing' rather than a person. But I loved that she got back on the sidelines and she will go forward."

Being captured on cell phones and videos certainly isn't limited to sideline personalities—college and professional athletes, team owners, you name it, have been caught by this new brand of citizen journalist who can record a seemingly private conversation at a restaurant and, before the ice in the drink is melted, post that conversation on the Internet. To that end, Lesley is helping young athletes understand their very public presence.

"The NFL, every couple of years, has me speak to the rookies, and they bring in former athletes and drug counselors. Sometimes I speak for the media, and that's when I tell these guys a couple of things: Number one, if you are respectful toward the media, you cannot imagine how that will help you. I always tell them, it's not a coincidence that the people who are respectful and have interesting things to say are the people who go on to the major jobs in television. We have Dan Marino at CBS, we have Boomer Esiason, we have Phil Sims.

"The other thing I tell them is, you just cannot underestimate that everybody is watching, and everybody is chronicling your life. And even for Dick [her husband, sportscaster Dick Stockton] and me, we go home long before the party's over."

The party is far from over on Lesley's career. She continues to cover network sports with the expertise and class she brought to the business out of Boston College. She offers her own advice for young girls and women who want to follow her into the profession: "There are two kinds of women who do what we do. There are women who love sports and they end up in TV, and then there are women who wanted to be on TV and they ended up in sports. And if you want to have a long career, a career that you are proud of, that other people are proud of, it's better if you have the passion first. We didn't do this to become famous. We did it because we love sports."

Another tip: "Turn the sound down [on the games] and what do you see for yourself? Do you see what the quarterback is trying to do with the receiver or with the running back? Do you see, in basketball, a college basketball game, can you see it's a zone or man to man? Don't just keep the sound up and listen to what the announcer's telling you. See what you can see for yourself."

She's knocked down doors, she's paved the way, and she's already inspired a generation of women in sports, garnering praise from colleagues such as Gayle Sierens, the first woman to call play-by-play for a televised NFL game. "She is just an inspiration to me, and I think to every woman who has ever been [in the business]," Gayle said. "She started as a newspaper reporter and writer, and she's just a true journalist who has hopped over all those obstacles—I'm sure she would tell you not always easily—but she's done it. And she is, I think, just a shining light in the world of sports for women."

chapter 4

Women in the Booth

"What a weekend! On the sidelines for high school football Friday night, sideline reporter for the University of Cincinnati Saturday night, and in the press box for the Bengals on Sunday. Thanks, Mom, for teaching me to be a sports fan."

—My Facebook entry, September 14, 2009

So here I am, getting ready to work the sidelines for the University of Cincinnati-South East Missouri State football broadcast during the 2009 season, and I have college football on the TV in the background.

First game I watch, I see my former ESPN colleague Cara Capuano on the sidelines of the SEC game of the week. Then I flip over and see another ex-ESPN colleague, my buddy Pam Ward, back in the booth this season doing play-by-play for the Michigan State game.

Cool, I thought, all three of us working games on this big college football Saturday.

And it would have been cool, if it hadn't been so ironic.

Because just the day before, I talked with Gayle Sierens.

For those of us who grew up watching sports, Gayle Sierens is right up there with Neil Armstrong when it comes to blazing trails. The difference: While Armstrong was followed on the moon by eleven other men, Gayle Sierens hasn't been followed by anyone. She is the only woman to call play-by-play for an NFL game.

Not that she had a career goal of heading into the booth, at least not at the time the call came in. But she did have a love of sports that got her to that booth. "I'm an only child whose father was killed in an accident when I was six, so I lived with my mother and grandmother. And they were gigantic sports fans. My mother loved the Miami Dolphins, my grandmother was a big baseball fan, so I came by that honestly."

Gayle also was active in sports. "I always participated in sports, primarily as a swimmer, but in high school, it was pre-Title IX, so those opportunities weren't the same as they are for young women today. But I was always interested in sports, and I lived in an environment of women who were very interested in sports, so it seemed very natural to me.

"I had one of those moms who said all the magic words: 'Do whatever you want, be whoever you want to be, I'll support you no matter what you decide.' But no one was happier when I made that career path toward sports."

Gayle Sierens

Gayle eventually went to school at Florida State University, where she got her degree in mass communications and got her first TV experience at Tallahassee. That led her to WFLA-TV in Tampa, where she started on weekend sports. Eventually she made her way to the prime-time sports anchor job, and in 1984 picked up a Florida Emmy Award for sports reporting while becoming one of the most popular personalities on the NBC affiliate. She also did some freelancing for ESPN during that time, but as far as a long-term career on the network level in sports, Gayle didn't see that happening.

"At that stage of the game," Gayle said, "at least at the national level, the women who were doing sports often weren't women who had made their way up through the trenches as sports reporters. And frankly, I didn't see any hope that I was going to have those kind of opportunities anytime soon."

So when her station asked Gayle to move from sports into news, she took them up on the offer. In October of 1985, after nine years in sports, Gayle became the prime time news anchor for WFLA-TV as the station wanted to take advantage of her popularity with viewers.

So imagine how she felt, a few months after settling into her new news anchor job, when she got the call from the then-executive director of NBC Sports, Michael Weisman, asking her to consider doing play-by-play for an NFL game. Weisman, who had a tape of Gayle's sports work, later reflected, "I wanted to break that glass ceiling."

"Michael is one of those guys who's not afraid to step out," Gayle said. "He is a risk taker as a producer. He did the game without the announcers, [December 1980, between the Jets and Dolphins] and everyone says, 'Oh, what a gimmick.' But I think he genuinely believed that it was time for women to break into sports at a bigger level. And I think he went in search of two or three of us who he thought might be possible candidates for that. And then we all trained with Marty Glickman [former athlete and sportscaster who, at the time, was NBC's on-air talent coach]. And they made their decision about who it was going to be, and I was the lucky person."

In fact, Leandra Reilly also was considered for the job, even to the point of calling a practice game. Later, she said, "I was never really in the hunt," although she got her chances a few months later when, on Valentine's Day in 1988, she called an NBA game between New Jersey and Philadelphia, the first woman to do play-by-play in the NBA.

When NBC made the announcement that Gayle would call an NFL game, that's when her preparation really started. Because she was a news anchor now, not sports, she was a bit removed from the day-to-day of the NFL. "I wasn't following sports the way I did when I was a day-to-day sports reporter. I didn't live and breathe every sports publication, every game that was on the TV. So I had some catching up to do. That made me a little nervous.

"The one thing I knew all through the process, though, was that Marty Glickman who was, God rest his soul, a wonderful,

wonderful sports announcer and fabulous human being, he wasn't going to let me fail. He was going to get me prepared. He was going to tell me everything I needed to know, and he was going to make sure that I was very clear about it, going into it.

"What added to all of this, I had just gotten married in September, I had become pregnant in October, so when I did this game in December, I was newly married, two months pregnant, and my life was pretty darn crazy at that point. The phone never stopped ringing for the period of about a month leading up to the game. It was not a time of a lot of sleep."

Her game would be on December 27, 1987, in Kansas City, between the Chiefs and Seattle Seahawks, calling the game along with analyst Dave Rowe. But remember, she was working in Tampa, home of the Buccaneers. Wouldn't it have made sense for her to call a game for a team with which she was familiar? Perhaps, except her bosses at WFLA wanted her to make history away from home.

"It was the only way that my company would agree to it. Because you have to walk in their shoes a little bit, too. Here they had this woman whom they had just asked to be their news anchor, who was trying to make this transition from sports into news, they were trying to get people in our market to forget that I was the sports chick, and look at me as their anchorwoman. They had spent a lot of money and promotion just trying to change what people thought of me.

"So they were a little reluctant about this, and frankly they could have said no, but they were gracious enough to say yes. 'We know that this was a dream of yours, and we certainly are not going to stand in the way of this opportunity, but after this is over, we have to talk. We have to find out where your heart really is.' But they did not want [the game] to be seen locally for that reason."

That's why Gayle had to board a plane during the holidays to call the game in Kansas City. During the pregame show, NBC's Bob Costas asked her about claims that her position in the booth was, indeed, a gimmick. "It will be proved a gimmick if I come out and fail terribly today," she said.

So what does she remember about that history-making day? "A lot of it is a blur," she said. "But here's what I remember. I remember it was cold, really cold, and I'm a Florida girl, lived here in Florida all my life, so that gave me an extra little edge that morning. I remember that I was in a booth that was surrounded by glass windows, that had about four people deep all the way around it, watching me—reporters—watching what I was doing. And that was very odd as a journalist, to be the person who was getting reported on, instead of doing the reporting, so I remember thinking that this is really not my element here.

"I remember the game just going so fast, like everything about it seemed to go so fast. I had done my charts, I was ready to go with my spotting charts, and on the opening kickoff of the game I called the wrong person. I knew who the person was, but my spotter misidentified him, and I didn't have enough confidence to go with what I knew because I thought, 'Oh, it must be me, I must be the wrong one.'

"And it was the wrong person and I thought, 'Oh, here we go, I can just hear the roar of people now saying, "She has no business being in that booth, why is she getting this opportunity?"' But everything settled down after that, and I said, 'You prepared for this, you know who these players are, you know what they're doing.'

"There were some interesting plays. They had offensive linemen running balls, they'd have offensive linemen eligible, and

I'm thinking, you know, I think these coaches are just throwing some of this stuff in to test me. But it was fabulous. It was a great experience and I look back on it with great appreciation for the process, how hard I worked and how hard Marty Glickman and the folks at NBC worked to get me to that point, and I have great and fond memories of it.

"There are always those times that I stop and think, 'Should I have done more?' But I would have had to make a very big decision to do that. NBC had asked me to come back and do six games the following year. Basically, if I had done that, I would have more than likely had to give up my job in Tampa. You know, timing in life is everything. I just started a family, and I had a steady job with a good paycheck. At that point, I had given birth to my first child, and the timing wasn't right.

"I couldn't work Monday through Friday, hop on planes on Saturday, do football games on Sunday. Truthfully, it would have still been at that point, where what they were offering me couldn't have paid my bills. So it would have been a huge gamble. If I was a twenty-something or an unmarried thirty-something person, I would have rolled the dice in a heartbeat. But that wasn't where I was in life at that point.

"So that was the decision. I have zero regrets that I chose my life that I have now, and my family, over that. But it would have been fun to see where it would have gone. And that's just something I'll never know."

What she did know, though, was her efforts were hardly unnoticed. The next day, an article in the *Orlando Sentinel* began, "Gayle Sierens was a huge success Sunday afternoon." Not a bad lead. "I would have to say that it was 97 percent positive and 3 percent negative," she said. "Truly, everyone wanted me to succeed. I even sensed that from most of the reporters.

"The biggest obstacle was that there were a lot of guys out there saying, 'How comes she gets this chance? I've been doing high school play-by-play, and then I did some college play-by-play, and why wasn't I next in line? Because she's just a woman and blah, blah, blah. But to put it into perspective, we don't get those opportunities to do high school games. Or to do college games. So if there was going to be a breakthrough, it had to be a big breakthrough. And we did have the breakthrough, and yet look where it's gone. There's not been another woman to do it."

But Gayle is confident that women will get an opportunity to follow her into the NFL, and soon. "The example I always use when I talk about this is Pam Ward's doing play-by-play in the Big Ten. She's great. She does a terrific job. And why they haven't given her that opportunity is just beyond me. I think it has to be coming. I don't think they can deny a talent like hers.

"And let's look at what's happening in the world of news. Katie Couric is anchoring an evening news. Diane Sawyer is anchoring an evening newscast. It used to be that people didn't want women giving them news about the war or what was going on in the world. That has changed dramatically from that standpoint. If it can happen in news, for the love of God, why can it not happen in sports? Is that a more important venue somehow than the people who are telling us what's going on in our world? I just have to believe that the time is near. I'd be very disappointed if it isn't."

Will it take a female sports executive to make the decision to move the next woman into the NFL play-by-play seat? Perhaps, Gayle says, but not necessarily. "I think there are men in place who can make that call right now, can and should, and maybe will. But I think [the issue] is getting a lot of attention. I hope we don't have to wait for these female executives, but it may take that. But I don't think so.

"Now I just think that for the good of the networks, they need to get more women involved in these top jobs, because we bring a different perspective to the table. And if you want your audience to grow, you need as many different perspectives as you can get. And I don't think that the world of sports has done a great job of inviting that element in. Let's just get a different view, instead of the good ol' boy idea of the way of doing things."

However long it takes for the second woman to call an NFL game, the record will always show that Gayle Sierens was the first. She let a lot of young girls [and men] see that it could be done, and could be done successfully. She took the heat, she took the pressure, and she succeeded, making it easier for that second woman to follow.

"I just hope and pray that it's not going to be a long time," Gayle said. "I truly in my heart of hearts believe that the time is near. I just think that the networks have to figure this out. And I think they will."

...

So if ESPN's Pam Ward is the next Gayle Sierens, Pam has the advantage of more than a decade's experience in the football broadcast booth. Pam and I became friends, almost by default, as the only two female anchors during the first few months of ESPNews. (Pam was there for the launch, I came five months later—and by the way, she is one of the funniest people around and immediately made me feel welcome.) But before that, she had play-by-play experience on a local level. "I went to the University of Maryland, then just started out at a small radio station on the Eastern Shore of Maryland, and eventually worked my way up to doing sports radio in Cleveland, then Washington D.C., then Baltimore, then ESPNews was born and I came up there.

"But when I was in D.C., that's where I started doing play-by-play on local radio. George Mason University was the first to hire me to do local broadcasts, and I kind of parlayed that into a part-time gig with ESPN. When they hired me full time in 1996, the caveat when I signed was that I would be allowed to keep doing it. And fortunately, because it's a lot more fun, I was able to parlay that now into pretty much exclusively doing play-by-play for them."

Sounds simple, but the process of moving from the desk to full-time play-by-play work wasn't quite that smooth. "Back in 2000 there was a column in USA Today, and the whole gist was that women were just sideline reporters. And reading that got me—it got me fired up. So I guess in a convoluted way, I have Rudy Martzke to thank for it, because he wrote the column.

"I got all fired up, took a walk, practiced [what I was going to say], and went into John Walsh [executive editor of ESPN] and told him that I wanted to do football. And I dramatically threw the newspaper down on his desk and said, 'I don't want to have to read this anymore. I want to be able to do football.' And he looked at me for about two seconds and said, 'OK, we'll make that happen.' So it was surprisingly—I wouldn't say easy—but it was something that happened pretty quickly after that. And I got three games in 2000, about eight the year after that. John Walsh and Steve Anderson were the guys who really got it in motion. But it was just going in and asking, and to my great surprise and delight, they said yes."

So, it's one thing to get the approval from the front office to actually do the game. It's quite another to prepare for the game, as Pam found out. But she got some great help just down the hall to get her started. "I went to [ESPN anchor/play-by-play man] Mike Tirico, who fortunately was still working in Bristol at the time, and asked him how he prepared, which was both a good and a bad thing because football is totally different from basketball. I didn't think it would be that difficult to prepare, but if you just think about it, you're talking about maybe eighty guys who play on a team verses when you do basketball, maybe ten will play. So just do the math and times that, and that's the preparation.

"He basically showed me how he prepares, but he prepares like nobody's business. So I looked at the way he did things, and I kind of oversaturated myself with information. Since then I've pared down.

"That first game was Toledo hosting Bowling Green, the day before Thanksgiving in 2000. I was so busy leading up to it, preparing, that I didn't have the chance to be nervous. But I guess when the day came, I just felt a little—I would say nervous would be the word. I didn't have butterflies or anything, but I knew that it was just a challenge for me. I didn't want to think too much about 'Hey, I'm the first woman to do that' because I think that would have been paralyzing. It was fun in a way, but certainly it was sort of a wakeup call because it really is so different from basketball, and it really took me two or three years even to learn how to efficiently prepare for a game, to loosen up on the air."

Over the years Pam has moved seamlessly from Mid-American Conference games to the Big Ten package, to bowl games. And she says the acceptance of her role has been more or less universal. "I have had absolutely no pushback from coaches that I've dealt with, and I know I've talked to people at ESPN, and they say that at the beginning they were flooded with people wanting to know basically what the heck was going on. Any time I made a mistake it was like the apocalypse, but when you listen to other guys, and they'll make a slipup, nobody even notices. But all that has certainly died down from the people at ESPN, who tell me there's little to no pushback, compared to other play-by-play announcers that they get feedback on.

"But a couple of coaches just mentioned it to me like, I remember Bobby Williams, the coach at Michigan State at the time. We sat down at the [pregame] meeting, and toward the end he looked at me and said, 'Hmmm, you're doing play-by-play, huh?' And I said, 'Yes, Coach, I am.' And he was shaking his head, kind of processing it, but nothing ever got back to me.

"And now that I've been doing the Big Ten for so many years, that's really helped. The coaches know me, and I've actually had coaches pull me aside and tell me that their daughters are really excited because they love football. I think there is a trickle-down impact, that the daughters of coaches are excited to see that they can be involved [in football] in some way. And I've had coaches pull me aside and also tell me they think I'm doing a really good job, which means a lot."

So if Gayle Sierens thinks Pam Ward is the next female in line to call NFL games, who does Pam Ward think will be the next

Pam Ward

to follow her in the play-by-play chair? That's not a simple question. "The problem is, there are not a lot of play-by-play jobs out there. And there aren't a lot of women doing it in the lower levels, and that's where it has to start. That's where we all get our training.

"I was fortunate. I was able to do some play-by-play at the University of Maryland, and also in my first radio job in tiny little Cambridge, Maryland, where I was probably talking to myself. But we need people in the lower levels, all these mom-and-pop radio stations, to give those opportunities, and that's really difficult.

"If you're doing, let's say, basketball, and there are more and more women doing play-by-play for women's college basketball, it's not a big jump at all for men to go from calling basketball to football, to hockey, to whatever. But with women, it is a big deal. I think this has to start at a local level, and then you work your way up to ESPN, doing probably basketball. Then, what you have to do, is tell your boss that this is what you want to do. Because otherwise they would never think of it."

But Pam thinks play-by-play doesn't seem to be on a lot of young women's radar screens—yet. "When I do these college games, I do have broadcasting students come up to me, and I would say, nineteen times out of twenty, they want to be sideline reporters. That's basically what they are seeing. Those are where the jobs are for women—most sideline reporters are women, even though those jobs are becoming more and more scarce.

"But I just tell the kids, the very, very few who want to do play-by-play, if you're going to college, get on your college radio station, get a tape and just listen to yourself. Because with all due respect to universities, your theory classes aren't going to do you any good. You just have to go in there and get it done and put something on tape. And then, a lot of it is luck and timing and being at the right place at the right time. But mostly I think you've got to really, really, really, really want to do it, and not just think, 'Hey, I think I'll do this.' Just because you've been in broadcasting a long time, you don't just snap your fingers and get a good job, a good-paying job. It's not all glitz and glamour, it's a lot of hard work, and there's a lot of luck involved in it.

"And if you don't really love it and really want to do it and really understand that you might have to move to a town that is not the greatest place in the world to live and you're not going to make any money, if you don't have that dedication, then you should go do something a little bit normal."

But because a newspaper article triggered Pam to ask for, and get, an opportunity to do football play-by-play, Pam has, in turn, given other women an opportunity to follow her—some day. "I've been called a trailblazer, but I think in order to be a trailblazer there has to be somebody else behind you on the trail. And so far there hasn't been a lot of people. But I would hope so. I think women doing play-by-play has become a little bit more, not necessarily acceptable, but something that's not abnormal anymore. Which is good."

chapter 5

Women Sports Reporters

"If there are hurdles in your way, jump over them."

—*USA Today* sports columnist Christine Brennan

The first time I met Christine Brennan was during the media tour prior to the 1996 Olympics in Atlanta. We were on the bus to visit some of the outlying venues to be used at the Summer Games—cycling, sailing, and the like. I knew her only by reputation, but seeing her on the bus validated our trip: Hey, if Christine Brennan's joining us, this MUST be a big deal!

The second time we met, when we actually got to chat, was at the Association for Women in Sports Media (AWSM) convention in Philadelphia in 2009. A five-minute introduction in the hallway turned into twenty minutes rehashing our lives, our careers, and our golf games. Her passion for what she does as a columnist for *USA Today*, and her commitment to women in sports media, are visible in everything she does, bringing their stories and causes to light. I wish I had a fraction of her energy.

That's certainly been a hallmark of Christine's career—if she's involved, then it must be important. Just look at a portion of her sports resume:

Christine Brennan

Sportswriter at the *Miami Herald*; Washington Redskins beat writer at the *Washington Post*; Olympic reporter since the 1984 Los Angeles games. Her *USA Today* column in 2002 on the lack of women members at Augusta National, home of the Masters golf tournament, fired up Martha Burke, who sent a letter to then-Augusta National chair Hootie Johnson and started a national debate on equal rights versus private clubs. She's written seven books so far, has won the Women Sports Foundation's journalism award four times, and was the first president of AWSM. It's an impressive list. And it all started back home in Toledo, Ohio, when her dad allowed her, even encouraged her, to play sports.

"My dad said I was happy playing sports," Christine said. "He said, 'We watched you, we could see how much you loved running and throwing and jumping and playing with the kids, especially with the boys, and they wanted to play with you. We just encouraged that. You were a happy kid and we just said, keep on doing that.'

"And I asked him, 'Did people look and stare? Because this was so weird. I was the tomboy of the neighborhood, but the only one. It wasn't like now where every house has two or three girls playing sports. I tell people, picture every field that you drive by. Every sports field, everything. Back in the sixties and seventies, all boys. You would not have seen a girl on the field. But that was our world. It's the stunning, wonderful, dramatic, fabulous changes due to Title IX in this country. Girls are getting a chance to play sports and be empowered through sports.

"But my dad was like, 'Hey, if other people thought we were weird, who cares?' He didn't care. He went out, got me a baseball mitt for my eighth birthday, what did the neighbors think? He went out, got me a bat, made sure I had all the stuff. We played catch, threw the ball, and played running bases all evening after he'd get home from work.

"He was so far ahead of his time, I tell a lot of folks, especially the more conservative crowd I speak with, my dad was a rock-ribbed Republican, but I learned early on not to stereotype. He was Mr. Republican, who was probably the biggest feminist I ever met. How about that?"

Her early years with her father are chronicled in her terrific book *The Best Seat in the House*, tracing the journey her father took her through sports as the oldest of four children, from playing ball in the yard to attending games at the University of Toledo, to watching Ohio State-Michigan at the "Big House" in Ann Arbor. Her love of sports, and love of journalism, led her to Northwestern University for bachelor's and master's degrees, and eventually to her first job as a sports reporter.

"This was in the early 1980s when I started at the *Miami Herald* covering the Florida Gators. So it's 1981, I'm twenty-three, just out of Northwestern. The *Miami Herald* was talking to the Gators, Charlie Pell was the coach back then, and they (the team) are saying, 'We don't want her in the locker room.' I had to stand outside.

"So how about this? The largest paper covering the Florida Gators, the most prestigious paper, its reporter, who happens to be female, is barred from going in to get the interviews to do her job. That didn't last long, because Charlie Pell soon was beckoning me to come on in. But I think that proves a point. We played by their rules. We could have slapped a lawsuit on them. I had the wonderful support at the *Herald*, the *Washington Post*, and *USA Today* of the men and women, including Katherine Graham at the *Post*, who led those papers to say, hey, we're with you.

"So I was never standing alone. And often some male reporters came and joined me and said, 'Hey, if you can't go in, I won't go in either. And I would do the same for a male reporter if it ever happened. But it was not in my nature to file a lawsuit. I was so thrilled to have my job, I was so honored, and still am. I love what I'm doing every day. So the *Herald* said, back in '81 with the Gators, let's just play it by ear and see how it goes. We would monitor the quotes, we would see what the other papers had, made sure we were not getting scooped. And within a half a season, the Gators were saying, 'Come on in and we'll work this out. Keep your eyes closed and we'd have some fun laughs about it.

"And I think that's the way to do it. I tell students to keep a sense of humor. This is not a funny issue. This is about access to your job, but there are moments when you just have to smile or laugh, never taking yourself too seriously. That's certainly the way I felt about the locker room issue, and it resolved itself, with the wonderful help of the *Miami Herald* and *Washington Post* leadership, within a couple of years."

...

Locker room issues were nothing new to another famed sportswriter, Selena Roberts, who is probably best known for her years at the *New York Times* sports department, and most recently as senior writer and one of the back-page columnists for *Sports Illustrated*, and as the author of *A-Rod: The Many Lives of Alex Rodriguez*. She's a five-time recipient of Associated Press Sports Editors honors. She has also won the New York State Associated Press prize for columns (in 2007) and numerous other awards for her sports reporting. But before all the accolades, she was a college student, covering football in the Southeastern Conference for the *Huntsville Times*.

"It certainly was a different time and place," said Roberts. "It was the late 1980s, and so there weren't a lot of gals around covering college sports. I worked for the *Auburn Plainsman*. I was the sports editor there. And the challenges weren't so much with the players, because I think the players had grown up certainly in an early Title IX era, where they did share facilities with women. They shared the basketball court with the girls, so I don't think it was the players so much.

"But you dealt with coaches who were not used to it. You dealt with athletic directors who were not used to it. So you had to cut a few deals to try to get players away from the locker room, because the locker room was forbidden territory back then. You had to make sure that you talked to a guy as he got off the court. Sometimes I ran down corridors to make sure I got a guy before he disappeared on me into the locker room.

"So you did a lot more chasing back then than you have to do now, but that was just sort of the way of the world. And certainly there was some resistance, but again it wasn't so much players as it was really just the old guard who ran the business."

Her career has taken her from Huntsville to the *Tampa Tribune*, covering preps and small-college sports; the *Orlando Sentinel* covering the Orlando Magic, NASCAR, and the Tampa Bay Buccaneers; beat writer for the Minnesota Vikings at the *Minneapolis Star-Tribune*; and a variety of assignments and columns during her dozen years at the *New York Times* before heading for *Sports Illustrated*. But sometimes, as Roberts has learned, the more times change, the more they stay the same, as she relayed a story from her days in Huntsville:

"I covered minor league baseball when I was an intern in college, and I worked there a little bit right after my internship ended. And there was this one moment with the Huntsville Stars, who were the minor league team back then. Most times, it was great, there was no problem, and then there was this one time when they were kind of playing a little bit of a prank.

"The players directed me toward a hallway, and the next thing you know, they had a little fun, and they got me kind of wet with a shower head. So that was one of those moments when they were having fun and having a good time. Actually, they were on a winning streak, so I think in the celebration somebody yelled, 'wet T-shirt contest' or something like that.

"It was one of those gags that, it's funny now, but at the time I was just like, 'what am I doing in this business?' But you know what? You get over it, and you're just fine with it, and certainly it was not a harmful thing they were doing, they were just playing a prank. So stuff like that comes up once in a while, but that was long ago."

Much more recent was the backlash Roberts received during her research into the Alex Rodriguez book that started as a profile for *Sports Illustrated* and grew into a headline-making book, revealing Rodriguez's use of performance-enhancing drugs during his time with the Texas Rangers. For years, Rodriguez denied using performance-enhancing drugs. But *SI* found out he was on a list of 104 players who tested positive during baseball's 2003 survey.

Just before the *Sports Illustrated* article was released, she confronted Rodriguez in person with the information she and *SI* colleague David Epstein had discovered—that he had tested positive for anabolic steroids in those supposedly confidential drug tests in 2003. Those results were supposed to remain anonymous, but federal agents seized the records and samples from baseball's contractors in April 2004 during raids in connection with the BALCO probe in San Francisco. Although the agents originally had search warrants for the records of ten players, they discovered the broader records and came back with additional search warrants. Names from those drug tests have been leaked in drips and drops— and that's how Rodriguez's name surfaced.

"As you know, even after we had all the information we did, I

still went down to Miami, I still
walked up to Alex Rodriguez, and
asked him about the 2003 test.
And we still gave him two more
days after that to talk to us some
more. Because at the time, he
referred us to the [players'] union.
While we went to the union, we
gave Alex another couple of days
to see if there was an explanation

Selena Roberts

for it. Could it have been a mistake? Could it have been a wrong
test? Could there have been something he had taken that screwed
up the test?

"Anything he wanted to say, he had an opportunity to say it.
Certainly after two days passed, we alerted him and his people that
we were going to run the story. And I think that's kind of where
the rubber meets the road. It isn't some sort of epiphany moment,
it's just a process of making sure you're absolutely right. Because
you know this is huge news. It was a huge, damaging moment for
him, and he's a human being, so you treat it as delicately as you can
because you realize this is going to rock everything that we know
about him."

After the *SI* story was released, Rodriguez finally responded two
days later in an interview with ESPN's Peter Gammons, in which
he admitted he had taken a banned substance during his days with
the Rangers. And then he went after Roberts herself, accusing her
of stalking him and claiming she had been thrown out of his New
York apartment; saying she had been thrown out of the University

of Miami weight room where she confronted him on his drug use; and trying to break into his house at Miami Beach.

None of which was true, and for which Rodriguez offered, according to Roberts, a clumsy apology by phone a few days later, as she writes in the *A-Rod* epilogue: "There were several things he neglected to apologize for, including his misogynistic stalker accusation and the trespassing whopper."

Here's some of what A-Rod said to ESPN: "This lady is coming out with all these allegations, all these lies, because she's writing an article for *Sports Illustrated* and she's coming out with a book in May. And really respectable journalists are following this lady off the cliff. And following her lead. And that to me is unfortunate."

After the article and the book were published, Roberts found herself defending her work, instead of promoting it. In the wake of Rodriguez's ESPN interview, Roberts told the *New York Observer*: "I think I was saying to myself, 'That's a really interesting take on what just happened.' It's not at all close to what happened. I wrote it off: It's a diversionary tactic to throw blame on the messenger. He's probably upset with me and maybe he wants to divert the attention to the credibility of the article, which is not in dispute."

Nevertheless, A-Rod's criticism of Roberts and the article became fodder for the bloggers of the world, coming up with such blog titles as "Why I Hate Selena Roberts" and "Selena Roberts Strikes Again." Would a male sportswriter have received that much criticism, especially the personal attacks? The question certainly is up for debate. One thing is for sure, though: While Roberts collected criticism, Rodriguez collected a World Series ring at the end of the 2009 season.

Suddenly a blast from a showerhead in a minor league locker room doesn't seem so bad.

...

Christine Brennan herself has been no stranger to criticism. Her move to *USA Today* as a sports columnist was any writer's dream—to have a forum in which to express opinions. However, her opinions on women's sports, Tiger Woods, and, yes, even the Erin Andrews incident, have made her a target of less-than-flattering comments. Criticism aside, she is forceful in her advice to other young women who want to be sports journalists. "Never pay attention to the naysayers. If someone says no, ignore that. Someone says you can't do it, just pay no attention. If someone says this is not for you or you can't do it, you can't make enough money doing it—if this is something you love, follow your heart, follow your passion.

"Nothing would have sounded stranger for me than to say I wanted to be a sports journalist growing up. It would have sounded more logical for me to say I wanted to walk on the moon. People in Toledo would have gone, 'Yeah, you can walk on the moon, sure you could be an astronaut.' I never read a woman's sports byline… so there's no logical way to say I'd end up doing this. And yet I have.

"There were no role models for me, and now, of course, these young women have hundreds of wonderful role models. They can say, 'Hey, I can do that because I'm listening to her, I'm reading her, I'm watching her,' and that's the beauty of this.

"So it's just simply this: If there are hurdles in your way, jump over them, work harder than anybody else, do not make mistakes, double check the spelling of every name, double check the score, be a perfectionist, and follow your heart and your passion.

"What worked in 1929 and 1959 and 1999 will work in 2029 as well, and those are the basic tenets that your mom and dad tell you. They're true and they're right. Just be so knowledgeable on the subject that no one can ever doubt you. And no one can say you don't belong because you are so prepared, whether it's baseball statistics or football or Olympic statistics, whatever it is.

"So put all that together, just the passion and all of its various forms that loving sports can bring, and then, of course, the love of writing and journalism or whatever the medium is. Just make sure that you're good enough at it that you can take advantage of it when the job opportunities open up."

chapter 6

A League of Their Own

"I think we need more women in powerful positions."
> —Orthopaedic surgeon Dr. Michelle Andrews,
> first female to serve as an MLB team physician

ou never know where sports may lead you. In the case of Michelle Andrews, it led her to the clubhouse of the Baltimore Orioles as the first female team physician for a Major League Baseball team. Now, I had known Dr. Andrews through her involvement in the Women Sports Foundation and its local chapter in the Greater Cincinnati-Northern Kentucky area. But she's also known as one of the top sports surgeons in the country. Being an MLB groundbreaker wasn't necessarily a goal for Dr. Andrews, but instead became a natural progression of her medical career.

"I've always been active and I've always played sports," said Michelle. "In high school I played, from ninth grade on. I lettered in softball and basketball, field hockey, and then I went to the University of Massachusetts and played field hockey and softball."

In fact, sports almost became her profession, instead of medicine. "I always wanted to be

Dr. Michelle Andrews

a physician, and I always wanted to be a surgeon. And I only had one time when I vacillated from that—and that was when I was trying to decide if I'd go to college. I was coaching little girls in basketball and I got such a kick out of coaching these kids, I almost decided to go into coaching, and my thought was to be an Olympic coach for field hockey. I finally decided I had to do medicine, but all along I've been very active with sports and spent a lot of time with athletes, so it just kind of fell together. But I always knew I wanted to be a surgeon."

So once Michelle knew she wanted to be a surgeon, the next question was, what kind of surgeon? The answer came in medical school. "It was just incredible to spend time with orthopaedic surgeons, because they were the happiest residents. You had to tag along as a medical student and watch how they did their medicine and how they did their life, and they were the happiest. They were a lot of fun. They were mostly ex-jocks, and they just had a great attitude, great humor, and were always active. And so I looked at them and said, 'This obviously is where I have to be.'

"The only time I think I had a little concern was—I'd always heard from the guys that you can't do it. But I did hear from one woman physician in medical school that I couldn't do it, which actually was a little more important to me than if I'd heard it from a hundred guys. Fortunately, I did have one mentor in medical school, it was a woman, who said yes, you can do it, don't listen to her."

Why did the one doctor say that Michelle couldn't do it? "I think it was probably that it was a grueling process. I mean, you're on call every other night, and it's not a very cushy job. It's a physical job—to put a total knee replacement in is a very physical job. I'm not necessarily a very big person, but I'm a very strong person. Most of the orthopaedic surgeons tend to be six feet tall, and a lot of them are ex-football players, so I think when you think of orthopaedic surgeons, you sometimes think of that type of person."

So Michelle followed her mentor, and her passion, and decided to go into orthopaedics. Among others, she studied under Dr. Mary Ann Keenan, one of the first women in orthopaedic surgery. "Back then it was very unusual [to have a woman in orthopaedics] because women as orthopaedic surgeons, it's less than 3 percent," Michelle said. "There used to be about 17,000 board-certified orthopaedic surgeons, and around 350 were women—so a little less than 3 percent, even in the good years."

Coming out of training, which included stints at Yale and a fellowship at her current professional residence, Cincinnati

SportsMedicine, Michelle was looking for her first job. "My goal was to go into academics. Since I was from Massachusetts, I thought that I would end up in the Boston system, perhaps Harvard. So I took a job at Johns Hopkins [in Baltimore], thinking I'd be there for just a short period of time. I was offered that job by an incredible man, Dick Stauffer [who at the time was Chairman and Director of the Department of Orthopaedic Surgery at Johns Hopkins University School of Medicine]. I said to him that I thought it would be appropriate, in my job as a sports medicine physician, to cover a Major League Baseball team or a major sports team.

"And so he looked at me, and you could see the wheels going, but I let it be, and I just let him know that it was something I thought would be very important to have happen. He said 'Let me work on it,' and he came back a couple of weeks later and said, 'You're in.'"

With those words, Dr. Michelle Andrews made baseball history as the first female to be an MLB team doctor. Sounds like an easy process, but it wasn't quite as simple as it seemed. "You had to be voted on by the owners and had to be voted on by the manager," Michelle said. "Then you actually had to be voted on by the players to see if you could come into the locker room.

"And so the first night that I went down to the locker room, I thought, 'Boy, this is gonna be fun; let's see what happens when I open these doors.' So I'm going through the doors, and the first person who meets me is Cal Ripken Jr., and he says to me, in his incredible class and style, 'Welcome to the Baltimore Orioles.' Being the team leader, obviously, he set the tone.

"I probably got more press than some of the players, because there was a lot of interest that I was a female physician for the Orioles. It was a lot of fun, I really enjoyed it, and there were a lot of great times being with that team."

So Ripken may have set the tone, but what was the feeling from the rest of the team? Did Michelle sense any resentment or resistance from them? "I think there was absolutely nothing that I felt to the contrary. I was definitely welcomed right from the beginning. Now, whatever happened along the way, before I walked in, I'll never know. But I can tell you that from day one, it was a lot of fun. I was truly accepted and it was not a problem at all."

She spent the 1993 season with the Orioles, while at the same time serving as team physician for Bryn Mawr High School and Johns Hopkins University's athletic teams. After the season, she returned to Cincinnati SportsMedicine as a partner physician. So, what if she had chosen coaching instead of medicine? Michelle says there's not much difference. "I am a coach. When I take a person through a total knee replacement, or an ACL surgery, or a rotator cuff surgery, what I do is prepare them. So it's just like any coach preparing them for the game. I lay out the plan, I tell them what the anatomy is, what's been injured, how we want to accomplish this, why it's important to work together. Then we go into surgery and I'm right there with them, and half the time they'll look up from the bed and say, 'Where's Dr. Andrews?' and I'll say, 'I'm right here.' So they know that I'm in the room from start to finish, that it's definitely a personal service that I give to each and every one of my patients.

"When I finish the surgery, I spend time with the family, I tell them exactly what I did, and then the most important thing—

now I'm a cheerleader. I worked really hard for you, I did a really outstanding operation for you, it went perfectly, and now, you have to be the one to buckle down and do the therapy. Because the bottom line is, if you want a good result, you have to work as hard as I just worked, so that we can both be happy with this."

And a lot of that is possible, Michelle says, because she works with athletes. "I think that an athlete, somebody in sports, who is truly committed to sports and knows what it takes, is probably a little bit easier to mentor through a tough operation. But it all comes down to personality. I think one of the gifts that I have is that I'm able to pick out personalities pretty well, and sense what is needed to make everybody a winner. You know you just can't leave the last one on the bench. You have to make sure everybody's on board."

But not everybody could overcome the obstacles, like Michelle did, to be the first to make sports history. "The first thing is, you have to believe in yourself. There has to be a very strong inner core to anything that you decide to do. And I think that comes from sports—that's what you learn in sports. I also think it's very important to seek out people who will support you. Now, you don't have to have everybody support you, you don't have to have a love fest, but you have to have someone whom you know, on tough days, that you can ask, 'Am I doing the right thing?' or 'What do you think about this patient?' or 'Am I on the right course?' You always have to have a sounding board to make sure that your values are staying the way they should.

"You also have to set your sights on exactly where you want to go. You have to be goal oriented. I have five-year plans, three-year plans, six-month plans, and weekly plans. You have to write it down, you have to say, 'This is what I want, and this is how I'm going to get it.' You have to have an energy, or a drive, in you that you're willing to go ahead and maybe miss a meal, maybe you're up all night in an emergency room, and not let it get to you. It's like doing situps. You may want to do ninety, but you're at eighty-five and you've got to put your mind somewhere else to get the extra five."

Michelle may have been the first female team physician in Major League Baseball, but she hopes she won't be the only one in that kind of leadership role. "I think we need more women in powerful positions," she said. "I think the world needs it, not just our country. I think there have been some shining examples of that in the world. I think women have the answer to a lot of the world's problems."

...

While Michelle grew up in sports-rich Massachusetts, baseball GM-to-be Kari Rumfield grew up in the small community of Hazen, North Dakota, where the closest Major League Baseball team was the Minnesota Twins. "Huge Twins fan," said Kari. "My grandfather would take me to Twins games, back when Kent Hrbek and Kirby Puckett played. I really enjoyed going to the baseball games. I was the first grandchild, so I was probably treated a little more special because I was the first one. My grandfather would always take me along, and even though I was a girl, I'd be right there with him, or he'd listen to it on the radio or TV and I'd be right there, so I really grew up enjoying baseball."

And that love of the game took her to the playing field. "I was in a small town that didn't have a softball team, so I played Legion baseball with the boys. I found that extremely difficult in the beginning, because it's not typically a girls' game. I played second base, but then, of course, I got to play a lot of outfield because I was probably one of the weaker links on the team. I wasn't very good, but I just loved being out there. I loved being part of that group sport. It took some time for everyone to accept me, but once they did, I was one of their teammates. Same with the community. It was a very small community, but it was something they just accepted.

So, her teammates accepted her—how about the parents of her teammates? Or the opposing players? "You know, I never really dealt with the parents of the players all that much. Once the players did take to me, though, they became very protective. Because when you're playing an opposing team, the other players would say things, but my teammates would always stick up for me. They became my extended family and my brothers."

So, sounds as if Kari was setting up for a career in sports. Well, it happened eventually—but not before a detour to Tennessee. "Baseball was only one of the things I was interested in," she said. "I graduated early from high school, graduated as a junior, and I was always ahead in math and I had a great knack for cooking and I had a great knack for arguing. So my father tried to push me toward becoming a lawyer. So when I first went to college, I really was going to school to be a lawyer. Then after about two years I decided I didn't want to do that anymore. That's not my passion. My passion was sports and my passion was food. So then I thought, well, I'm going to go down the path of becoming a registered dietician and go to culinary school. I loved cooking. I still love to do it, it's still one of my biggest passions, and I thought, 'This is what I'm going to do.' And then I decided, well, I'm going to take some

Kari Rumfield with husband Toby

time off from school, go travel, do some things, and I ended up in Tennessee, starting off as a waitress and then a bartender."

Kari's venture into the food profession took her to Starbucks and Outback Steakhouse and, eventually, to her future husband. "I was doing the whole life thing, seeing if I could figure out what I wanted to do with my life. That's when I met my husband, and that's how I got involved in the whole baseball thing."

She got involved because her husband, Toby, was in AA baseball with the Chattanooga Lookouts, then an affiliate with the Cincinnati Reds. "The team had one p.m. games on Sundays, home games, and when they were done, they would come into the restaurant to eat. The wife of one of the pitchers, Chad Fox, [who won a 2003 World Series ring as a member of the Florida Marlins] was one of my employees. So she had introduced us at some point, and we became friends. He was never really my type. He was quiet, he was a cowboy from Texas, polite, very nice guy, but just really wasn't my type. There was nothing romantic about that connection, but a year later, there was, when he came back."

And that's when they shared another love—of baseball. "I never really spent a whole lot of time talking to Toby about baseball. It wasn't until that connection of the romance that he really understood that I was pretty intelligent when it came to that sport, and that I really liked it. It was all she wrote after that—the whirlwind romance, the marriage, and then babies.

"When Toby finished playing in 2003, we were both struggling to figure out what we wanted to do with our lives. We had just had our third child that really wasn't planned—we had planned on having two—and he had just finished up a year where, he had a great year, but was trying to figure out where he wanted to go. Did he want to continue to play, which he could have done, or should he go into coaching or managing?

"Just so happens that he had sent out his resume to several teams in the area and the San Angelo Colts, it's a West Texas town, the owner there wanted to meet with him about managing his baseball team." Toby got the job, and Toby, Kari, and the three babies packed up and moved to Texas. "We got moved there, I'm staying at home, and I was talking with the owner one day, and he said, 'How would you like to sell advertising for us part-time? You can do this from home.' I'm thinking to myself, I don't know about this, and he said, 'Do you have a fear of calling people on the phone?' And I said no, not really. But I had no idea what I was doing. I knew baseball, and I knew all the promotions, and I knew there was more [to sell] than just the game. But I never really paid as much attention to all that until he said, 'Would you do this?' and I said, 'OK, what am I selling?'

"So he hands me some sheets of collateral and says, 'Here's our sign prices, here's the program prices, here's this, here's that' and I still didn't know what I was doing. I was on the phone with these people, and I had no idea what I was selling. But I was setting up meetings with people. It was about building that relationship. Well, within a month he hired me full time because I had sold so much, I had so many prospects out there, that he already figured he was going to pay me way more than it was worth to just hire me full time. So that's how I got my first job in baseball."

As with most baseball jobs, if you want to get a promotion, you often have to move to get it. That's how it worked for the Rumfields, when Toby got a job with the Kansas City Royals as a scout, and the family moved to the Chicago area. But by this time, Kari had the baseball bug. "There just so happened to be a position open with the Joliet Jackhammers [of the independent Northern League]. It was a corporate sales position, and I got the job. And I learned more in those two years when I was with the Jackhammers than I did all my years in baseball.

"There were two women there, Kelly Sufka and Sara Heff, one was promotions [Heff] and one was the assistant general manager [Sufka] at the time, and these two had worked with other teams as well. And among the three of us, we were really a force to be reckoned with. Because we would come up with such great ideas and we did a lot of networking together, it was really a great team to work with. I'd come back and say, 'OK, Heritage Bank is interested in this, but I've got a mind block. This is who he's trying to reach, this is what he's trying to do, and all of a sudden between the two of them, they'd come up with all these great ideas, and I'd go, 'That's it!' You always want to come back with that great idea and not the traditional advertising."

For example, here's an idea that certainly doesn't fit the "traditional" mold: "A couple of years ago in River City we had a company called The Three Blind Guys. It's a window blind company. They sponsored the umpires. It was hilarious. Because we'd always say, 'Tonight's umpires are brought to you by The Three Blind Guys.' Now, we did get permission from the commissioner—the umpires are very sensitive individuals."

But after a couple of seasons, in true baseball tradition, it was time to pack up again. "I spent two years with them, and then I was promoted, because the general manager [of the Jackhammers] bought a team in River City, outside St. Louis. He promoted me [to assistant general manager] and moved us down to St. Louis. He also hired my husband as his manager. I was there for a year. A lot of things were new to me there, because I had never done retail buying before, and I had never done the promotional buying before. I had never put together the promotional schedule all by myself. Here were all these things I was being thrown into, but I loved the challenge."

Then halfway through the 2007 season, she got a call from Clint Brown, the new owner of the independent Frontier League's Florence Freedom team, based just outside Cincinnati. "He said, 'I'd love to interview you, I've heard great things about you, would you come to Florence?' And I'm thinking, oh my gosh, I'd have to move again. You know I'm packing my kids and we're dragging them everywhere. So I came to Florence and met with Clint and things really clicked. So that's how I got to be a general manager."

One of a very few female general managers in baseball, at any level. "The last time I checked there were less than a dozen," Kari said. "Obviously people get promoted, people move on and decide that's just not for them, but that's about right."

And the reason some women decide it's not for them may have its roots in the very culture of the game. "To say baseball is an industry governed by the old men network would be probably an understatement. There are still a lot of people in the industry that think a man can do a better job, think a man should know the game better than a woman.

"When I go to meetings, winter meetings for baseball, and I'm being introduced to different people—'Hey, this is Kari Rumfield, she's the general manager for the Florence Freedom'—people will say, 'Oh my God, you're a general manager for a baseball team? I still meet general managers of major league clubs, and their jobs are a little bit different than mine, but they're just blown away by that.

"Now, where it gets a little uncomfortable for me is, I think there are a lot of times men in this industry look at me and say—I hate to say this, but it's there, it's like the elephant in the room—she's blonde, she's pretty, how did she get her job? I still think there's some of that there until they realize, 'Wow, she really is smart.'

"I was named the Frontier League Executive of the Year [in 2009], and that wasn't because I was blonde and pretty. It was because I was smart and I knew what I was doing. And I think I don't try to feed into that a whole lot, I just kind of bypass it. Once my mouth opens and I start talking to them, I think it's then that the light goes on and they say OK. I don't think that's with everybody, I just think that the industry is what it is."

And there's an added element to her general manager's job with the Florence Freedom: Her husband, Toby, is now the team's field manager. So, in effect, Kari is her husband's boss. So how does that work out at home? "He's an easy person to work with,'" said

Kari. "It's not that hard. It's not like I have to tell him, well, you do this and you do that. I never have to pull the 'I'm the boss' card. He understands that having the community involved here is very important, so he comes in and does selling for us and he'll go out and speak to schools, he'll go out to organizations that want him to come out and speak. He understands that being a part of all that only makes us stronger. He's really good about keeping me in the loop, and I'm really good about respecting the fact that he has a job to do. And his job is to put together a very competitive team.

"Now, during the season, when he pulls out the closer and brings someone else in and they score two runs and they win, I do question those moves. I say, 'Why would you bring that guy in? Why would you do that?' And he gets a little mad, but I think I have a right. As the general manager when I see stuff like that happen, and I ask him that, he does get defensive, but I said, 'I'm asking you this as the general manager. I'm not asking you this as the wife. I want to know why you did that, because we lost because of it. So I want to hear your thoughts on it.' And he'll be like, 'You're right. This is why I did it. You're right, he didn't do a good job.'"

But while baseball may be the family profession, Kari also realizes that she is very fortunate to be making a living in a game she loves. "I think that life is too short to just go to work every day and not be happy, and not have a passion for what you're doing. When I go into retail places or restaurants, I always think, 'If you don't want to be here, then don't be here. But while you're here, you should do the best job you can possibly do.' If you're the dishwasher, I think you should be the best dishwasher you can possibly be.

"Coming to the field every day, I've had people I've worked with for years here, and every once in a while, I have to remind them of where they're at, and what they're doing. Because they'll get into that slump and they get a little burned out, and I'll have to stop them and say, 'You need to decide. Is this what you want to do? Because if you don't want to do this, then you need to find a job that you can be happy with. And I want you to remember what you have every day. You come to a ballpark every day. You get to spend months meeting with people, talking to people, talking about baseball.

"'You're not selling a vacuum cleaner; you're selling a baseball ticket. You're selling entertainment. You're selling a fun promotion. Granted, not everybody's going to want to do your fun promotion, but you're going to meet some great people. Yeah, in the summertime, you don't have a social life and you work all the time. But look at all the great playing time you get now, look at all the great things that get to happen, things we get to do.'"

While Kari gets to do something she loves, she admits that, for other women it's not going to be easy to do what she's doing. "As a woman I would say, and it sounds bad, but you need to work harder than the man. You've got to prove to the people above you that you really want the job. If that means that you're there earlier than everyone else and later than everyone else to get the job done, that's probably what you're going to have to do.

"I would say that internships are one of the biggest ways people get hired. For example, we just hired a new business manager, and he was an intern with us, starting last January. Unpaid, January to September, thirty years old, he's got two master's degrees, he's an incredible, hard-working individual who earned the position. I've learned that between the known versus the unknown, I'll take the people I know. Because I know what their work ethic is already.

"Be very persistent in getting what you want. You are probably going to have to start at the bottom to work your way up, but here I am, an example of starting at the bottom and being at the top within a couple of years. I think as a woman it is possible."

...

Kari already has the title of general manager; Kim Ng doesn't have it yet, but she just may become the first woman to hold that title in the major leagues. She's already worked for two of baseball's iconic franchises, the New York Yankees and the Los Angeles Dodgers, while building an impressive management track record of her own in her job as assistant general manager for the Dodgers.

Ng is one of only three women (with Jean Afterman of the Yankees and Elaine Weddington Steward of the Red Sox) ever to hold the title of assistant general manager in Major League Baseball. She's interviewed for general manager's jobs numerous times and now runs the Dodgers' day-to-day operations. In the age of computer-savvy, college-educated GMs, she fits the new mold of baseball executives. And it all started with her love of the sport when she was growing up in New York.

"I was such a tomboy, it wasn't even funny," said Kim. "I had scabs on my knees, mud running down my legs all the time, you couldn't get me in the bathtub. I pretty much had a ball and a glove in my hand, or some kind of ball anyway, or a racket. So I grew up loving sports.

"Growing up in Queens [she was born in Indianapolis], we just didn't have the big outdoors like they do in some parts of the country, but we played a lot of running bases and a lot of stickball. I guess I shouldn't admit this too loudly, but I was a big Yankee fan as a kid. My favorite player was Thurman Munson. My dad was a baseball fan, but the sport that he truly loved was football. But for some reason I just was drawn to the game."

She graduated from high school in New Jersey, then returned to the Midwest to study public policy at the University of Chicago, where she played softball and first got the idea that maybe she could make a living out of sports. "The first time that it actually occurred to me was when I was a senior in college. I started doing my thesis paper on Title IX, and I just thoroughly enjoyed the research and talking to the people, knowing that my school had such a great rich history in women's sports. I really began to wonder if I could make a living out of it."

An internship with the Chicago White Sox helped her wonder no more. "When I got that internship, it wasn't a ton of money, but nonetheless, I was still getting my foot in the door, making me realize that maybe I could make a go of it."

The internship turned into a six-year tour with the White Sox, becoming an assistant director of baseball operations. She entered Major League Baseball at a time when clubs were looking for statisticians and research specialists in the age of *Moneyball*, the Michael M. Lewis book about how the low-budget Oakland A's used research and development to find baseball bargains. Her research experience and baseball's changing dynamics gave Kim a once-in-a-lifetime career opportunity.

"I think the advent of computers in baseball, looking at things in a different way, being able to analyze problems and problem solve, I think helped me to get my foot in the door and has had a great effect throughout my career. I came in at a great time with a new TV deal with Major League Baseball—there was a lot of money, and they needed analytic people to help them in the front offices. So I was lucky to come in at the front end of the whole movement."

She then spent a year working in the American League front office before she returned to New York as the assistant general manager for Brian Cashman at the Yankees. "I learned a ton there," she said. "That's when I really sort of got into the nitty gritty and understood how decisions were made—there, anyway. And I really got a feel for how different people think about the business of baseball and a professional sport. Brian Cashman was a great mentor to me. And it was really fascinating to see the way Mr. [George] Steinbrenner thought about things. Unorthodox, very much so, but nonetheless, it worked. I'm not sure how you dispute five trips to the World Series in six years."

Working for her favorite team for four years gave her the background, and the opportunity, to take on another legendary franchise, the Los Angeles Dodgers, again as an assistant GM, first under Danny Evans, then Paul DePodesta and Ned Colletti. She's run the farm system, managed the scouting system, and handled arbitration cases. In other words, she's done just about everything dealing with daily club operations. Other clubs, other baseball executives, have taken notice of her chances to become MLB's first female general manager.

"I don't think the group is exclusionary," Pam Gardner, the president of business operations for the Houston Astros, told Yahoo! Sports. "I think the group is ready and open for it. If you're in an environment with open, smart, and confident people, then women are welcome. It takes a confident group to embrace a woman."

DePodesta has called her "smart, tough, and strong." Evans hired her twice, in Chicago and Los Angeles. Afterman, who followed Ng in the Yankee front office, said of the GM hiring issue: "I think it's more difficult for an outsider to be accepted than it is a gender issue. And Kim is an insider."

Ng echoes that opinion. "I've been accepted very well. I don't think you get to a position like mine and say that you've been disrespected many times. For that I'm really grateful and very, very, fortunate, especially with all the people who have helped me throughout my career. I look back and think, 'Gosh, how did I get here?' I'm very respectful of the people who came before me, of the game itself, and what these guys do on an everyday basis. It's been very rewarding for me, and, again, I'm very appreciative of everything I've been fortunate to achieve."

One incident still shows that not everyone is as accepting: Former big league pitcher Bill Singer, at the time a special assistant with the Mets, ran into Ng during baseball's general managers' meetings in Phoenix, asked who she was, why she was there, and what her heritage was. She answered his questions patiently, and then he answered in what was supposed to pass as Chinese gibberish.

She saw it more as an assault on her gender than her Chinese heritage. He blamed it on the alcohol. After meeting with Ng and both clubs, Singer was dismissed. Everyone who saw the incident said Ng handled it with as much poise as possible—it's something she is reluctant to discuss, even now, but did tell Yahoo! Sports it was an example of what one incident could do for her career. "I couldn't believe I was in the wrong place at the wrong time, and that now I could be seen in this completely different light. I believe I take great care with what I do and how I behave."

With all the success she's achieved in baseball, was there anyone who tried to talk her out of this career? Well, yes, surprisingly.

"That was my mom," Ng laughed. "Coming out of the University of Chicago she definitely wanted me to pursue my MBA, my MD, she would have been thrilled to death if I went to medical school. Parents just have this very orthodox way of thinking about their kids and aren't necessarily willing to think out of the box. So when I came to her with this, she was not pleased. But by the time I had worked my way into a job that paid me a little bit more money, I think she was OK with it."

Her various stops in baseball have put her in the offices of some of the strongest leaders in MLB, and she says she's been able to glean something from just about all of them. "Each of my bosses, in their own way, has been a mentor to me," she said. "But everybody has a different style—it's like being at the salad buffet, you get to pick which works for you. Certainly [Dodgers General Manager] Ned Colletti, who I work for now, Brian Cashman, and [former Dodgers GM] Dan Evans. Of course, [former White Sox GM] Ron Schueler, my first boss, Jack Gould, the minority owner of the White Sox, and Mr. Steinbrenner, to a certain degree. Mr. Bob Bailey, who owns the Dodgers with Frank McCourt. It's been a lot of fun and seeing the way that different people think, it's been so valuable to me."

It's not often that any of us gets to work for a legendary company, group, or franchise, much less two. Ng has had that opportunity, and the responsibility is not lost on her. "There are so many things I've been fortunate to experience, and being with two storied franchises is certainly at the top of the list," she said. "When I think about the people that I've come across throughout my career, having worked for these two clubs, Graig Nettles, Ron

Guidry, Don Mattingly, who's been at both places, Maury Wills, all these great, great players, it really is amazing. It really is.

And one of the things that the Dodgers are very well known for, is being a pioneer internationally, and that's actually something that I take a lot of pride in. It's something that goes back years and years, something that Mr. [Walter] O'Malley, the O'Malley family, was very committed to, and I see that now. And it's nice to know that certain things just don't die, and that there are great traditions that we as an organization uphold."

Ng already has GM interviews under her belt, and for better or worse, teams tend to go through general managers like hitters go through broken bats. So the opportunities could be just around the corner for Ng to take the next step up the MLB management staircase. She's careful with her words, but leaves no doubt what her goal is.

"I think, just in terms of the [management] ladder and natural progression, you'd like to think so. But in terms of whether it does happen or not, nobody knows. I have no idea. I try to really focus on the job at hand and what's in front of me. First and foremost, it's trying to get us [the Dodgers] to the World Series this year.

"The way I've always conducted myself is if I do a good job, if I do a very good job, good things will happen. And it's definitely been true throughout my career, and hopefully we just keep continuing on and getting better here."

There are those, even in L.A., who think Ng's time is right. Jeanie Buss, vice president of business operations for the NBA Lakers, [owned by her father, Jerry Buss] told Yahoo! Sports Kim's chances depend on the organization, and those above and below the office of general manager. "I want to see in my time frame a successful female GM in one of the major leagues," she said. "It's going to be tough. I don't know Kim personally, but from what I know, she really does things the right way. She knows her job; she's done the work. She deserves an opportunity."

It's an opportunity Kim thinks that others should have down the road. Her advice? "I guess number one would be don't let anybody tell you what you can't do. Only you will determine that. And another thing is, you have to be absolutely persistent. I've had friends, male friends, who have taken eight internships to get their first full-time job. But it's about chasing your passion.

"With that, there's definitely some pain involved, but if you fight and you struggle and you pay your dues, hopefully that turns into something later. So I would say the most important thing is to be persistent."

chapter 7

The Business of Sports

"I like having women in charge."

—Tina Kunzer-Murphy, executive director,
Pioneer Las Vegas Bowl)

It may be Christmas Eve, but that hasn't stopped Tina Kunzer-Murphy's phone from ringing as I stop by her office off the Vegas strip. She's on her cell phone as she unlocks the office door, then answers the office phone when a sponsor calls, asking about a police report.

A police report?

"We took several of our clients to a football game in Oregon," she explains. "First thing, when they land, everyone's golf clubs disappear. Stolen. We're still trying to straighten that out."

Even though the Pioneer Las Vegas Bowl (now the Maaco Bowl Las Vegas) has wrapped up for 2007, Tina Kunzer-Murphy is still tying down loose ends and planning for the staff debriefing meeting scheduled for after the first of the year. As the executive director of her hometown bowl—the first female executive director of a major post-season college bowl, the game itself is

Tina Kunzer-Murphy

only a fraction of her responsibility. Sponsorships, partnerships, hospitality, all are part of the bowl experience that Tina oversees. And in 2010, she added to that the chairmanship of the Football Bowl Association, the first woman to take over that job. So how do you grow up with the ambition of being a big-time bowl executive director? Well, according to Tina, you don't.

"I wanted to be a dancer, so I did the dancer-cheerleader thing," she says. "Once I got into college [first at Southern Utah State College], I saw that dancing wasn't going to work out, so with Title IX going into effect, I played sports. I wasn't very good at anything, but I played everything."

She eventually transferred back home to UNLV, where she concentrated on tennis, then became the school's women's tennis coach when she graduated.

"We fought a lot of battles to get better uniforms, better equipment," she says. It wasn't easy, but I believe you take a job, and you make it what you want it to be. You're going to have a lot of crummy jobs along the way—it's up to you to turn them into something better."

Tina was quite happy turning the women's tennis coaching job into something better over her three years at the helm. That's when then-new UNLV Athletic Director Brad Rothermel called her into his office.

"He asked me, 'Have you ever considered being an assistant athletics director?' and I said 'No, I really like coaching.' He asked me again, 'You sure you've never thought about being an assistant AD?' And I said, 'No, not really.' Then he said, 'Well, you might want to reconsider because I'm dropping the women's tennis program.' So I thought for a second, then I said, 'You know, I've always wanted to be an assistant athletics director.'"

But there's a kicker to the story. "The best part is, once I became an administrator, I was able to eventually bring the women's tennis program back to UNLV," she smiles.

So began Tina's career in sports management, first at UNLV, then at Pacific, and then back to Las Vegas working with the city's minor league baseball and hockey teams. A job managing major championship events for the Western Athletic Conference eventually led her to running the Las Vegas Bowl.

The bowl itself is relatively new, with the first game, between Bowling Green and Nevada, played in 1992. A brainchild of the Las Vegas Convention & Visitors Authority, it was born out of the need to fill hotel rooms. "Believe it or not, with everything going on in Vegas, the one week that they're looking for tourists here is the week before Christmas," says Tina. "So to bring in out-of-towners during that slow period, the Visitors Authority came up with the bowl game."

And just like most every new bowl in the mega-bowl post-season lineup, the Las Vegas Bowl struggled in its first few years. Then, in 2001, sports giant ESPN bought the bowl game, their first bowl property, and brought in Tina to be the executive director. Since then, with a full-time bowl staff of only four, 40,000+ attendance has become the rule, not the exception.

"The facility [Sam Boyd Stadium, the home of the UNLV football Rebels] is a bit of a challenge, since we don't have access to selling the suites for the bowl game," Tina says. "So we have to be creative in how we make the hospitality experience the best we can offer."

For example, Tina and her staff wanted to offer a "suite like" hospitality experience without the suite. She first approached UNLV about going halves on auxiliary end-zone bleachers. It would have given fans an on-field experience, as well as made more tickets available for this sold-out event, the third straight year it had been sold out. But UNLV said no. So, it was time to get creative.

"We approached La-Z-Boy and came up with the idea to put up a huge tent in the end zone. Big La-Z-Boys inside and out facing the field, food, and flat-screens to watch the game," Tina smiles. "We sold 250 tickets at $250 apiece, another 200 at $150 each to go into the tent. Terrific addition, and sponsors loved it."

Not everyone loved every part of the 2007 Pioneer Las Vegas Bowl, though, as Tina produces a folder filled with printed-out emails from fans of both schools in the bowl, UCLA and BYU.

The 2007 Bowl had tie-ins with the Pac-10 and Mountain West conferences and the more it looked like the game would be a UCLA-BYU matchup, the more Tina tried to change it—you see, UCLA and BYU already had met in 2007, a 27–17 win at home for the Bruins.

"I really wanted to bring Boise State in," Tina says. The Broncos became the darlings of the bowl season with their thrilling 43–42 overtime victory against Oklahoma in the 2007 Tostitos Fiesta Bowl. Everyone, including Boise State, agreed to the change—everyone, except UCLA. So the Bruins, with their 6-6 record and an interim head coach, were coming to Las Vegas to face the 10-2 Cougars once again. Which did not make BYU fans happy.

"Look at these emails," Tina says, as she brings to her desk a file folder filled with pages upon pages of electronic fan vitriol. "They think I pick the matchups. I don't pick the matchups. We have an agreement with the conferences. The conferences and their schools make those decisions, but I get the blame.

"But you know what? I answered each and every one of these. And once I explained it, most people accepted the decision. I pride myself in making it right for everyone, and when you take pride in what you do, in what *we* do here, you usually can make people happy. At least they know the story on how the matchup came about."

As it turned out, the UCLA-BYU game was one of the most exciting in the bowl's history, coming down to a last-second UCLA field goal try that was blocked by BYU, handing the Cougars their second straight Las Vegas Bowl title and giving the game a 2.4 overnight rating, its highest ever.

"It's strange the way it works out," Tina says. "The whole week leading up to the game was a disaster, and the game turns out terrific. Last year, the week before the bowl game could not have gone smoother, and then the game was a blowout and ratings were below 2.0. So you never know."

Bowl Week activities, which Tina also supervises, include the official team welcome the Wednesday before the Saturday game, a children's hospital visit on Thursday, and a kickoff luncheon Friday with Bonnie Bernstein, the sideline reporter for Saturday's broadcast, as the featured speaker this particular year.

"I caught heat for having Bonnie do the luncheon, but you know why I picked her?" Tina asks. "Because I like having women in charge. I find that women can see the big picture, they can get organized and make it happen. I like to surround myself with successful people, from the bowl committee to staff."

Her father was a butcher, her mother, a waitress. Tina knew she loved sports and followed that passion to a career in sports management, at a time when very few women were in that profession. And she has found a way at every level to be successful, even when a change of athletic directors at UNLV forced her to look for other opportunities.

"You have to be willing to be rejected," she says. "You find out what you're made of and at the same time, you find out what other people think of you. Once you're fired, it forces you to look within yourself to know what you really want to do, and what you need to do to get it. I love working with people who've been fired, because they are centered—they have a special passion, a focus, and know what they want to accomplish."

And her advice to others who want to follow her path is simple. "Get your foot in the door, turn your job into the best job you can make it, and surround yourself with good people," she says. "We're lucky here in the bowl office, because it's a small staff, and I try to give recent graduates and interns an opportunity to learn the business. When you work through layers and layers of management at other businesses, it's not always so easy to get the experience you need. These students get to be around some of the most passionate people in the business when they work on this bowl game. And that passion is infectious.

"They also learn that I'll give them flexibility, but I also expect them to get their jobs done. They know that we may work four hours in the office on Wednesdays, but we'll work eighteen-hour days during Bowl Week. They learn how to be organized. They have to. If you don't manage your time well, you'll never get your job done.

"For women, it's a different day now. The opportunities are there, no matter what career you want to enter. Just remember three things: Follow the rules, be financially stable, and win. For us, winning means a successful Las Vegas Bowl. And every year, we work to make it more successful than the year before."

...

For Brigid DeVries, a walk through her offices at the Kentucky High School Athletic Association in Lexington, Kentucky, is a trip through a time machine. "I can remember in the office we had a mimeograph machine, and I can remember that we had one secretary that did the envelopes. Now, we email things out. We're like Mission Control here."

Before her retirement in 2010, Commissioner DeVries was one of only three women who were commissioners of high school athletic associations—New York and California being the others. Her commissioner's job is just the latest stop in a life that revolved around sports, even from an early age.

"My father was an excellent tennis player, and I'm from a tennis-playing family. In Lexington, at that point in time, the parks department had some very excellent programs, and that's where I learned to play tennis."

Tennis gave way to swimming and diving, participating in the Greater Lexington Swim Association. "My first real job, as a lifeguard, I was making $1.60 an hour, and I thought I was rich." Undergraduate school at the University of Kentucky led to a teaching job in physical education at a K-through-eight school, then back to U.K. for a master's degree.

"At the University of Kentucky at that time, you had to do intramural sports, you might have to teach a class, and you had to coach two sports," she said. "So I worked with volleyball one year, and I did track and field one time, and swimming and diving at the club level.

"I know they've changed a great deal, but college programs then were a great place to get a tremendous amount of experience. Now, a lot of it wasn't paid. You just volunteered, you got pulled into this or that, you officiated, you had to coach, and you were taught and mentored by other people. And so I got some really good background there, and as programs started to grow, being at the right place at the right time with the right background helped me probably get my foot in the door."

Brigid DeVries

The door opened for DeVries at the KHSAA after a three-year stint at Ohio University coaching track and field and swimming and diving. "They [the KHSAA] were looking for people that had Olympic sports background, and so I kind of fit the bill, and I've been here ever since."

So DeVries joined the KHSAA in 1979, first as an assistant commissioner running events, then as executive assistant commissioner in 1994. During that time she directed the organization's gender-equity program, conducted eligibility investigations, and assisted in management of the state football and basketball championships—and a lot more. "When I first came to the association, there was a commissioner and three assistants. Very small staff. We had four secretaries, now administrative assistants. No sports information. I ran the track meet, wrote the press release, mailed about ten of them, I called up T-shirt vendors—'I need 250 T-shirts and here's the artwork,' and had to proof it ten times, and at ten o'clock in the morning, it's 'Have you got those shirts over at the track, we're here and we don't have any.' You call up the vendor to set up for the event, so you had to do all that."

She took over as KHSAA Commissioner in 2002 with strong praise from her predecessor, Louis Stout, who, at her appointment, said, "She has the character, the professionalism, and the knowledge to sit, listen, evaluate, and make tough decisions."

"You have to be flexible enough to say, 'Hey, I'd like to do that,' who knows when that door will open," she said. "I know this—the door opens only a few times. And you have to be ready to jump through it. I have been happy ever since my very first teaching job, my first lifeguard job, my first age-group coaching swimming job, participating and playing in USTA tennis. Everything I've done, I've enjoyed. So it's just kind of a natural progression. I would have been just as happy as an assistant commissioner, but the door opened. And I thought, well, I'm jumping in."

So does being a woman help in her role as commissioner? "When you're the new person on the block, people are always looking at you like, 'What do you know about that, to be able to do that?' So you're constantly in 'I have to prove myself' mode.

"In other ways, women are very detail oriented. So if you're not detail oriented you'll get in trouble running those events. And I've always felt like, if we're going to do it, let's do it really well, or let's don't do it. When we first got going, some of our resources were limited, but we're still going to do it better than anybody. Especially when you get into state championships, you know what the statistics are for kids moving on and playing in college. This is probably the last sports experience they're going to get. In Kentucky we try to put the best venues out there for our kids to participate in, because that's going to be their only experience. And we want them to walk away from that and go, 'That was really special.'"

And for DeVries, the experience should be special throughout a high school student-athlete's career, no matter what their level of ability may be. "High school sports do it all. Some of the U.S. sports governing bodies, they're going to be able to spend more time and hire coaches that can train student athletes before school and after school that are moving on to the Olympic level. A high school program probably can't do all of that, but what it does do is gives all the participants an opportunity to do something for their community.

"In high school, you'll have the klutzy student athlete that rolls in who is part of the team, and then you'll have the elite level. And you're going to recognize them all. But there is a point in time when the elite-level child needs to go on and go professional, and let the rest of the average Joes have participation opportunities in high school.

"I had a parent call up one time and say, 'You know the dates of your state tennis tournament are going to give my daughter trouble, because she has the opportunity to play in the Junior French Open.' And I said, 'I think that's the most fantastic thing, but we're not changing our high school dates.' If someone's good enough to play in the French Open, go play in the French Open. And let Judy over here have the chance to be a state champion."

So what kind of advice does Commissioner DeVries give to young people, especially young women, who are pursuing jobs in sports management? "I've mentored a few students, and what's interesting is, what I always try to tell people is, have a goal and a dream. They may change from time to time, but I think a lot of students coming out of college make a mistake by limiting themselves. They say, well, I just want to stay where I am, but if you can't be flexible, if you can't travel where the opportunities are, you're making a big mistake You're going to have to: A, get out of your comfort zone, and B, you might have to take a job that's remotely related to what you want to do. But at the end of the day, you have to build a resume and get all the experience you possibly can.

"And the other point is, volunteer for stuff. This generation wants to be paid eight or ten dollars an hour, and they'll be looking at their watch when it's time to go. It's the ones who stay a little bit later, work a little bit longer that, in my opinion, are going places. I see people look at me when I tell them this like, are you kidding me? But that's my advice. And those who want to succeed, end up in those positions."

How DeVries ended up as Commissioner is a testament to her love of sports and her willingness to be open for any opportunity. "It's sort of an adventure. The only thing we try to do here is just to keep moving forward. You're going to have your detractors, you're going to have people that think they have all the suggestions in the world, but our thing is just to focus on the student-athlete, make that participation opportunity available for them, and keep moving forward.

"We've done some things that are very unique around the country, and for that, in a state like Kentucky, there are far more participation opportunities than there ever would have been. To me, for girls, I think the sky's the limit because good people are going to emerge. If you're thorough at what you do, people are going to need you."

. . .

To say soccer is Tonya Antonucci's life not only describes her day-to-day job, but also her athletic passion. Because no matter what field she's worked in, from software to new media, she's never strayed far from her soccer roots. No wonder, then, that she now has taken up

Tonya Antonucci

the task of relaunching women's pro soccer in the United States as commissioner of the Women's Professional Soccer League.

I first heard her speak at the Association for Women in Sports Media convention in Philadelphia, where her passion for the game of soccer, and her ideas in the use of new media to promote it, got the audience buzzing as she discussed the launch of the new women's soccer league.

"It was the perfect fit," said Antonucci, "I was in the right place at the right time to get involved."

How she got to the right place started with her love of soccer and a sports portfolio that's impressive by itself. She was a high school soccer All-America and a member of the 1984 U.S. Junior National Team. From there she played at Stanford, where she was a member of the All-Far West Team and co-captained the Cardinal her senior year.

When she graduated, the option of pro women's soccer wasn't available, but she stayed close to the game while working on her M.B.A. at Santa Clara University by helping coach the school's women's soccer team. After that, it was a journey into new media: She was a project manager at Starwave, the Paul Allen-backed Internet content company, then a content producer for a precursor of espn.com before she joined Yahoo, Inc., and launched Yahoo! Sports and its very popular Yahoo! Fantasy Sports. Wait a minute. A female launching not only a sports Web site but a fantasy Web site where, even now, only about 12 percent of the top participants are women?

"I guess I really didn't think twice about it," said Antonucci. "I felt that I was qualified and was going to work hard at it and had a vision for it and had convinced those around me that I had a path to be successful. And I think in the computer world, in the Internet space, there's a bit more of a level playing field. It's not a traditional kind of sports environment, offline sports environment, where it's a little harder to break in. The barriers just weren't there.

"Ironically, if anything," she continued, "it might have been harder to be an engineer in the Internet space. There just weren't as many female engineers. But in terms of being on the business and the product-media-marketing side of it, it really wasn't an issue. And I was very pleased with that, and it helped me continue to stay motivated and committed to what I was doing."

Antonucci spent more than seven years with Yahoo, Inc., eventually adding to her responsibilities the title of general manager of Yahoo's partnership with FIFA (Federation Internationale de Football Association) and overseeing the commercialization of the global Web sites for the 2002 FIFA men's and 2003 women's World Cups.

The next step in her career, though, came as much through happenstance as through planning. Two weeks after she left her job at Yahoo Sports, Antonucci went to a party for Stanford soccer alumni. At that party was one of her former teammates, Julie Foudy, who served as captain of the U.S. women's national team. By this time, the first incarnation of women's pro soccer, the WUSA, had come and gone, suspending operations in 2003. Julie wanted to see if a women's professional league could be revived.

"Julie asked me if I could focus on it, write a new business plan, and then go and try to find some investors who could get behind it and make a commitment to the league. And so I said, absolutely, Julie, I'll do it, did it in a heartbeat, haven't looked back.

"I've just always cared a lot about the game and its development. And when I saw that WUSA had closed its doors, I was really curious about what had gone wrong and how there could be a course correction and bring it back. After leaving Yahoo and looking around for a new startup—a new adventure because I love starting from the ground up and being the underdog—I said this was the right thing for me, and I want to take it on and work hard to learn the lessons and see if we could bring it back."

Antonucci first was the CEO of Women's Soccer Initiative, Inc. (WSII) for two-and-a-half years, during which time she did her due diligence on what didn't work for the WUSA and what could work for a new league. Much of the research started with the cost structure. "We looked at the WUSA and said, 'OK, they started out with an initial investment of $40 million, and they ended up spending about $100 million over three years.' They had such lightning in a bottle with the '99 Women's World Cup, our question was—how could they have spent less and sustained it?"

The 1999 FIFA Women's World Cup-winning team not only featured Julie Foudy but the face of U.S. women's soccer, Mia Hamm, the veteran Michelle Akers, and the *Sports Illustrated* cover girl,

Brandi Chastain. All household names coming out of the Olympics, all of them the idols of young soccer-playing girls across the country. If you can't make a women's league succeed with a lineup like that, how could you make it succeed? That was Antonucci's task.

"What we looked to do is see how we could bring those costs down, more in line with where the business would be in the early years, and grow and manage the business closely over time so there would be an audience and sponsorship and television.

"So we looked at the cost side: First and foremost were the stadiums. How do we play in facilities where the economics are better for our owners, and, of course, create an authentic, intimate soccer experience for our fans, a fun environment. But how do we bring those costs down?

"Another area was how can we take the staffing and front office approach and find ways to create efficiencies, and do some job sharing perhaps with another team—doesn't even have to be another professional soccer team. But where we can create partnerships and have others be invested in our success to help us establish a footing?

"And I guess on the revenue side, we just wanted to state more modest expectations so that the definition of success could grow, and we could grow into it and keep those costs in line. It was difficult to do, but there was a good basis for starting off. By that I mean, the WUSA closed its doors averaging between 4,500 and 5,000 fans per game. And we thought, you know what? That's a nice little league, that's a nice little business to start to put the world's best players back on the field."

So in March of 2009, this "nice little league" took the field with seven teams: Boston Breakers, Chicago Red Stars, FC Gold Pride, Los Angeles Sol, Saint Louis Athletica, Sky Blue FC, and the Washington Freedom. Members of the U.S. Women's National Team were dispersed among the teams in a 2008 draft, so name players would be on each team in each community. But Antonucci wants more than just a national audience watching her league: She's looking for an international following, and she brought in international stars to do it.

"Probably first and foremost on that list would be Marta, three-time FIFA World Player of the Year from Brazil. She's just been a dynamite player in our league. The players talk about her, the fans talk about her, she is a creative goal scorer, as fast as lightning, and some of the women and men who come out to watch our games say they haven't seen a player like her, ever, in person." Marta ended the inaugural 2009 season with ten goals, the top scorer in the league.

"I'd be remiss if I didn't also mention Kelly Smith, the best player out of England, playing for our Boston team, who, by the way, also played for the Philadelphia Charge of the WUSA, and Sonia Bompastor, a French international, who is just lighting it up on the field. She's so creative and skilled, and she's really helped take the Washington Freedom to second place now in our league." [Washington ended the season 8-7-5, in third place and in the playoffs for the inaugural league title, eventually won by Sky Blue FC.]

With Antonucci's background in new media, it is no surprise that she's taken that experience and turned it into a way to market her new league. "Let's face it," she said, "we're a young league without a big marketing budget, and social media is a way to directly connect to our fans in a low-cost manner. And our fans get a first-person account of what's going on."

That includes using the social media site Twitter to allow players to 'tweet' messages to their followers during the games. "You get the behind-the-scenes story, you get the emotion, and that's a really neat and unique connection.

"Now, our players who are in the game and playing on the field are certainly not 'tweeting,' but the occasional player on the bench, who is sharing some insight with fans following along, it's just a great tool. Now, who knows what the next 'thing' will be, but again, we want to make sure that we're kind of catching fans where they are in terms of their own communication tools."

Tonya Antonucci has taken her love of soccer and her expertise in new media and combined them to be the future of women's professional soccer in the U.S. Adding Philadelphia and Atlanta in the first round of expansion is the first step in growing the league, but Antonucci doesn't expect it to be the last step.

"I think in five years we'd like to have twelve teams in our league, to the extent that the player pool supports that. We certainly want to keep the quality at absolutely the highest, world-class level, so we will be mindful of that. We want to expand our national footprint and go into communities of soccer hotbeds where there's an audience that craves watching the sport, participating in the sport, and would sustain a team.

"We want to have audience numbers from 7,000 to maybe up to 10,000 fans per game. I think that is maybe slightly aggressive, but if we're shooting for between 4,000 and 6,000 now, which we are at this point achieving in our league because we're averaging about

5,400 fans per game, we're kind of in the wheelhouse there.

"I think we want to see probably five to six major top-brand national sponsors who are activating around our brand and working with us to grow awareness of the league. And I think we want to be in the forefront of what's happening in the digital space in terms of bringing our players, their personalities on and off the field, the game, to fans wherever they might be.

"The players are accessible, appreciative, and it's a fun sport. It is the best you will see."

chapter 8

Following Your Passion

"You have to have the drive to tackle something a little bit bigger than you."

—Zayra Calderon, LPGA

When Zayra Calderon was twelve, her father told her she had to stop playing soccer with her brothers because it wasn't ladylike.

Sue Enquist batted second on her high school's boys' baseball team. She led the league in getting hit by a pitch.

Sounds unbelievable, you say? How could a well-meaning father do that? How could pitchers get away with intentionally targeting another player? Well, they did, and somewhere they probably still do. Being cut out of, or discouraged from, sports has been, historically, the rule rather than the exception for millions of women and young girls.

Despite being discouraged from playing sports, Zayra Calderon went on to a successful corporate career before she found her passion in women's golf, first as the CEO of the women's developmental Futures Tour and then at the LPGA itself.

Sue Enquist brushed herself off, nursed the bruises, and took her batting skills to UCLA, where she played for the Bruins' softball team and then later took over as head coach. She owns eleven national championships as a player and coach.

What they have in common is what all the women in these chapters share: An unrelenting drive to succeed in sports, no matter who might say they don't belong. Their stories, while unique, have a familiar theme you'll find throughout these interviews: Passion and pride and unwavering belief that what you're doing is right.

...

Zayra Calderon's first glimpse of a golf course was through a fence and palm trees as she rode on a bumpy, dusty school bus.

The course, the pristine grass, the elite who played there, were just yards away. But to young Zayra, this seemingly privileged life might as well have been half a world removed.

So there was no way for her to know that she eventually would play on courses like this, do business on courses like this, and eventually make golf her passion, as well as her profession.

Zayra Calderon is the Chief Executive Officer of the LPGA's

Zayra Calderon

developmental tour. She is also the LPGA's Senior Vice President of New Business Development. I got to know her as CEO and owner of the Duramed FUTURES Tour, the official developmental tour of the LPGA. Pretty heady stuff for someone who grew up the youngest of ten children— five boys and five girls—in rural Costa Rica.

And just like many youngsters in this Central American country, she grew up playing soccer on her parents' farm. "We were all phenomenal dribblers, because we had to dodge cow patties," she said.

Of course, she played with her brothers—that was their recreation out in the country. But at the age of twelve, that life ended. "My father said I was getting too old, and I couldn't play with the boys any more," she said. Her brothers, of course, had no such restrictions. But Zayra thought her soccer days were over.

As you can imagine, it was a major adjustment for a young girl who had a passion for sports. So, she participated in more ladylike activities, like horseback riding and tennis. But her passion for soccer never went away.

Fast forward to 1971, when Zayra came to the United States to attend graduate school at the State University of New York. "One of the first things I saw on campus were girls playing soccer," she said. "Girls playing soccer! I was so thrilled! It was a club team, and when they had tryouts, I tried out and made the team. I wore the number 10 in honor of my family and told my mother, 'See, girls can play here!'"

The whole experience was rather overwhelming to Zayra. "When I first saw the girls play, I was absolutely fascinated and thrilled. They had uniforms, they were good, and they didn't have to hide."

And all those years she wasn't allowed to play organized sports? Well, she made up for it in graduate school. Not only did she play soccer, she joined the ski club, the running club, played tennis—if there was an activity, she did it. Along the way, she learned all the lessons that you pick up in sports: teamwork, taking direction, making quick decisions, being gracious whether you win or lose.

Zayra eventually earned her Ph.D. in psychology, was an associate professor at the University of Connecticut, then joined CIGNA Health Care for a twenty-year career, from personnel to human resources to CEO of CIGNA Dental Health and senior vice president of CIGNA International, Latin America Division. But it was her time at CIGNA that opened the door for her next profession, in golf.

"I started playing golf in 1990, because I learned that it was the way you did business. I needed to do business, so I learned golf." And it was when she was in Florida as CEO of CIGNA Dental that she learned about a developmental tour for golf, the FUTURES Tour, where young women played to get experience before they moved on to the LPGA Tour. She also learned that the FUTURES

Tour was in trouble, and one of the officials of the tour asked Zayra to get involved and put together a business plan.

"So Eloise Trainor [who founded the tour] came to my office that night with three boxes of profit-and-loss sheets, statements, records of revenue, you name it. She asked me to put together a pro forma financial statement of the business."

It took ten days, but Zayra took the tour's finances, spread them out, and put them back together. "What I found out," Zayra said, "is that it was broke, but it had a future, if it was directed the right way."

The entire plan came together at the intersection of Zayra's passion for sports and her knowledge of business—mixed with her psychology degree. She proposed having the LPGA designate the FUTURES Tour as the official developmental tour of the LPGA. Eloise would continue to run the day-to-day operations, while Zayra would take care of the business side, including trying to convince the LPGA to give this fledgling tour its blessing as the official developmental tour.

"I met with Jim Ritts [then the LPGA commissioner] at the Orlando Airport; I made a presentation to the LPGA's board of directors; and finally in 1999 the LPGA agreed to consider changing its constitution to designate the FUTURES Tour as the official developmental tour—pending a vote by the players."

And this is where the psychology degree came in. "Tracy Kerdyk [former LPGA player who by then was on the FUTURES Tour staff] and I talked with the players about the benefits of having this as the official developmental tour. That was the key to our success. Once we had the LPGA's blessing, the tour became legitimate, and much more attractive for young golfers to join and learn how to be professionals before moving on to the LPGA."

The rest, as they say, is history. Zayra eventually took over full ownership of the tour in 2000, and since then she negotiated purchase of the tour by the LPGA in July 2007, negotiated the award of LPGA tour cards to the top money winners on the tour's final money list, starting with three cards from 1999 to 2002, five cards from 2003 to 2007, and ten cards in 2008. The tour set a record season purse of just over $1.79 million in 2009, and enabled the tour to contribute more than $4.5 million to charities.

And with the LPGA's reorganization in late 2009, Zayra added the job of global sales and new business development for the LPGA at a time when the tour is looking more and more overseas for tournament stops and broadcast revenue. But it all goes back to her passion for sport and her drive to save a struggling golf tour for young women in central Florida.

"You don't do it alone, you need a team," Zayra said. "We salvaged the Tour by elevating it, but it's just the beginning. The aim is to open up some of the doors for these young women. We took it from a player saying, 'I have to play on the FUTURES Tour' to 'I'm proud I'm playing on the FUTURES Tour.' It's the level of recognition we've given to the tour and its players. It's no longer a place where these young women are learning to play golf—they know how."

Others in the world of golf are taking note of what Zayra has been able to do in her job with the LPGA. As the association re-organized itself after the departure of former commissioner Carolyn Bivens, one of the first jobs the new leadership took on was the mending of tournament fences—rebuilding relationships with long-time tournament sites and sponsors that couldn't afford to continue with new LPGA and television fees tacked on.

Much of that fence mending fell to Zayra, who was credited in a sports trade publication with reaching out to these tournaments to find a way to continue the relationship. "Calderon is trying to be flexible with the cost structure of an event, including fees tied to purses, television, sanctioning, scoring, and player services, which can run up to $5 million for a tournament owner," writes Jon Show with *Street and Smith's Sports Business Journal*. "That cost has roughly doubled from a few years ago at a time when tournament sponsorship revenue is down as much as 30 percent."

In the article, Calderon says, "We are making an effort to deliver a personal message, to look at these people in the eye and say, 'This is our situation. Tell me your situation, and let's figure it out.'"

And she received even more glowing reviews from *Golfweek*: "Calderon, a fast-talking Costa Rican who worked seven days a week since former commissioner Carolyn Bivens was ousted, predicted she'd deliver 25 events during a phone interview more than four months ago," writes Beth Ann Baldry. "The total number of events is down, but it's a solid start for Calderon and her team to build upon. She plans to put together a team of tournament hunters and deploy them to key markets around the country, instructing members to stay put until they've scoured under every stone. The hit-list: Phoenix, Colorado, Washington, D.C., Georgia and Florida."

So how do you get from the dirt roads of Costa Rica to a seat in LPGA management? Here's how Zayra did it: "You should have a fundamentally strong business background so you understand revenue, expenses, and profits. Especially when you're talking about the Tour, you're selling the invisible—intangibles. You have to start from the bottom up, and an internship is worth its weight in gold.

"Also, be realistic—don't go into a sport that you don't love or can't love. And you have to have the drive to tackle something that's a little bit bigger than you. That's the pepper in the recipe. You do it because you see something bigger, that you can make a difference. That is what fuels you."

. . .

Sue Enquist knew all the time what she wanted to do. "I was the tomboy with short hair that everybody thought was a boy," she said. "I played all the time. Grew up with my brother and all his buddies, and a lot of them just thought that I was one of the boys. And it was a great time. It was a wonderful time."

Even when she stood in the box against opposing pitchers who weren't so accepting of a girl playing on a boys' team. "I was the first girl [in the state] to play on a boys' high school baseball team [at San Clemente High School in California]. I batted number two, led the league in getting beaned. I think that's a nonverbal way of saying you really shouldn't be playing. But it was the greatest experience of my life, and also catapulted my opportunity to go to UCLA."

Sue is a dynamic presenter. I had the privilege of interviewing her before a speech at the Greater Cincinnati-Northern Kentucky Women's Sports Association awards dinner, where she talked about her passion for the sport and her drive to succeed, both as a player and as a coach.

Sue Enquist

In an interview during her coaching days with the Bruins, she said her own high school baseball coach helped her succeed. "Joe Claudy treated me like everyone else. He said, 'If you work hard and have the skills, you will get to play, and I'll take care of the heat.'"

She played on the junior varsity while her brother, Bill, played varsity. Coach Claudy made sure his players were treated fairly and all had the chance to play, and Enquist told womenssportsnet. com that her coach's attitude set the tone. "San Clemente had a huge impact on me. Guys took care of me and treated me like one of their own. I grew up surfing, and guys in the water treated me with respect. I built a lot of self-esteem. They taught me how to be tough, how to compete and not be a baby."

She went straight from San Clemente to the softball field at UCLA, but the transition wasn't as easy as you might imagine. "I had an academic counselor tell me I would never make it at UCLA. I always tell that story, so that student-athletes out there know they are capable of doing academic work.

"Maybe they're poor test takers. I was a poor test taker. But I got good grades. And I think that's what really enabled me to be successful at UCLA. I just really worked hard, I graduated from

UCLA, never left UCLA, continue to work there now part-time [in development]."

Her career became the stuff of legend in Westwood, becoming the program's first All-American and the most outstanding player of the 1978 AIAW Championships, the precursor to the NCAA championships for women, where UCLA won its first softball national championship. But it was the 1970s, when opportunities for female athletes were still slim.

"I remember my freshman year at UCLA—we didn't even have uniforms. We didn't have vehicles to travel to our away events, and we didn't have meal money, and we really were just kind of a club team hovering above intercollegiate status.

"When Title IX became active at UCLA, we were able to implement some things. Judith Holland, who was really the architect of women's athletics at UCLA, came in and got us those opportunities, and we never really looked back. And many other schools as well took advantage of the partnership with the NCAA, and pretty soon you started to see females getting opportunities, just like their male counterparts."

Remember, this was the time when UCLA basketball ruled the college landscape, and UCLA football was a regular in the Rose Bowl on New Year's Day. Enquist says the softball team was accepted on campus but not so much outside. "There was great camaraderie [among student-athletes]. We would share classes together and have social outings together. But society-wise, outside the campus environment, to the media, we were so second class. I can remember winning that first national title, and we were six, seven, eight pages deep in the newspaper.

"That was a little bit disheartening, but I learned something valuable when Judy Holland brought in all the editors of all our major newspapers in Southern California and had a roundtable. What resonated was, they basically said, we're in the business to sell papers. So if ping pong is popular, then we're putting ping pong on the cover of our sports page.

"And the lesson I learned is, we as females are not doing a good job of working together and being heard. We're good at recognizing when there are injustices, but we've got to pull together more, we've got to create those alliances more, reach out more to our fellow female colleagues. Because although we look at it as an opportunity to expand brands and expand sports, it's a business.

"We as females have to get the word out that if your female student-athletes are not getting the exposure, mom and dad and the student-athletes should call the newspaper. Because they respond based on who's calling, who's emailing. To them, it's a business. They want to sell papers."

Enquist moved from playing for UCLA (with a career batting average of .401) to coaching the Bruins' softball team with legendary results. She has won eleven national championships total, either as a player or coach. She's been inducted into the National Fastpitch Coaches Association Hall of Fame. She's been the Pac-10's Coach of the Year. She's coached twelve Gold Medal Olympians and fifty-eight All-Americans. Her winning percentage (.835) is in the top five on the NCAA's list of all-time winningest coaches. She not only has blazed a trail for other players and coaches to follow, she's made it a four-lane Southern California highway. And she is encouraged when others, especially young players, want to follow that route.

"The first thing is know, and identify, your guiding principals very early in your life. And that's simple: It's family, faith, school, and ball. Secondly, you've got to maintain the two things in life you can control, your effort and your attitude.

"Then you have to be strategic. You have to get to, and be a part of, organizations that are competitive, so your game can go to the top. Then you must be organized in your recruiting journey and find your fit with college so you can expand and grow and have a good experience.

"Then from there you forge those alliances so when it's time to graduate, you can reach out to other individuals who are in coaching. Then it's a matter of just knocking on doors, being a volunteer, showing that you're capable, leading other younger student-athletes beneath you. Then it's just about letting everyone know that you have a passion for it.

"Coaching has to be a passion. We're not going to be millionaires—yet—and you want to make sure that you're always doing something that you love. And then you never feel like you have a job."

chapter 9

They Call Her Coach

"You can't be afraid of failure and not being able to achieve."
—Bernadette Mattox, first female assistant coach
for a Division 1 men's basketball program

*I*f high school basketball was great for Jean
Dowell, then she figured college basketball would be even greater.
After all, the game had come pretty easily to her, as far back as she
could remember. "I started practicing when I was just a little child,"
Jean said. "When I was in second grade I couldn't wait to practice
basketball when I got home."

When it really clicked in, though, was in third grade. "I had an
older sister. She graduated from high school when I was in third

grade, but she was a cheerleader. And that didn't appeal to me at all, but I went to the games and saw the crowds, and I thought, gosh, I don't want to be a cheerleader; I want them to be cheering for me as I play!"

And so they did, at Union Grove High School in North Carolina, where Jean and her twin sister played. "She was very good, too," said Jean. "That kind of helped us sometimes to get a lot of publicity. One night our team scored seventy-one points in high school, and we scored all of them." Tragically, her twin was killed in a car accident Jean's freshman year in college.

T. Jean Dowell

Jean was known around the state for her play. She led the voting for All Conference three of her four seasons, averaged thirty points a game her senior year, and led the balloting for All State during her final year. She had more than 2,000 career points and had her uniform retired. "I was thinking this was wonderful, and I was very disappointed that my high school days were over, but I thought it's going to be so much fun to go to college and play."

The college she selected was Western Carolina, primarily for their programs in physical education, but there was just one problem when she got there: They didn't have a women's basketball team. "They had sports days and play days back then. They had intramurals, and I enjoyed it a lot, but I kept fighting for a team, saying, 'This isn't right. We've got to have a team.' There were other good players there, too, some of them All State. We loved playing, so we were always trying to get them to start a program.

"And so my senior year [1965–1966] was the first year for Western Carolina to have a women's basketball team. And I loved it. We didn't play that many games, but we were fairly successful. In fact, in that short period of time, I averaged 30 points a game, and nobody's ever broken that.

"A side note here: They used to have free throw contests for women. I would practice every day at Western, every day except Sunday when the gym wasn't open. I would make fifty in a row. If I missed on the forty-fifth one, I'd go back to the beginning. I'd make fifty in a row before I'd quit. And so one day I was down there getting ready for this contest, and I made 192 in a row and finished it up with 199 out of 200.

"So I go to the cafeteria, and all the football team and everybody was there, saying, 'She's the one, she did this [made the free throws].' The next day I went down to the gym, and there was this big crowd there, and they wanted me to shoot free throws, because they couldn't believe it. And I didn't want to do that, with all that pressure? Go out there and do this again? But I finally went out there and I made sixty-nine without missing, so they knew it was for real."

After graduation Jean taught one year at Thomasville High School in North Carolina before deciding to get her master's degree at the University of Georgia. Once again, she was going to a university that didn't have a women's basketball program. Once again, Jean made it her mission to try to get a team started in Athens.

"I went to the gym every day, I got to know the people there, and I was practicing all the time down at the gym, shooting free throws and shooting jump shots, and everybody was coming by to say, 'Hey look at this girl shoot, you can't believe this girl.' What I said back to them was, 'We need a girls' team; we need a women's team here.'

"Of course, they'd say, 'Oh, we can't do that.' And I said, 'Well, I don't understand why you take tuition from men and women and yet you only give the men the chance to play. It'd be the same as saying the women can't use the library. The women can't use any computers. You know it's not right; you know it's not just.'

"And so I kept on and kept on, and finally one day I was called in, and the secretary of the head of the [athletic] department said the chairman was in there waiting for me. And I went in, and they said, 'Hey, you can have a team next year. And we'd like for you to be the coach.'

"So I was really thrilled about it, because I thought, here's the start, here's the beginning. But I remember that secretary saying, 'Jean, you're the most aggravating thing we've ever seen around here. There's nothing we can do with you!'"

So Jean got her wish and organized, then coached, the first Georgia women's basketball teams in 1967–68 and 1968–69. While it was a big deal for Jean and the players, the team's arrival was not necessarily greeted on campus with a ticker-tape parade.

"They didn't even know we had [a team]," Jean admitted. "We put up signs everywhere, the players were excited, their parents were excited, their friends were excited. It took a long, long time. But ten, twenty years later, it's still like, does anybody know the women are playing today? Does anybody care that the women are playing? I always thought people would, if they just knew about it, if they got the same amount of publicity.

"The school decided we could have a team, but we had to buy our own shoes, buy our own food, all those kinds of things. It was long after Title IX in 1972 that all of those came along. But it was wonderful—we were absolutely thrilled about it." Her work would eventually help her win the Distinguished Alumni Award from the University of Georgia in 1990.

Jean, of course, had no idea that what she was starting at Georgia would become a legendary women's basketball powerhouse. As of the 2010 season, the Lady Bulldogs would boast twenty-six NCAA tournament appearances, five NCAA Final Fours, and four National Coach of the Year honors.

And so, two universities, two women's basketball programs started—Jean was two-for-two. But she wasn't finished playing yet. In 1968 she heard about an Atlanta AAU women's basketball team and had one of her old coaches make an introduction to the AAU coach. Problem was, the coach asked her to come down on a Tuesday night for a game. She had a class but wanted to try out, so she drove down anyway. She got there late.

"They were playing already, so I went up to the coach and said, 'I'm Jean Dowell.' He said, 'There's your uniform over there on the bench. Go in and get changed.' So I came back out, it was the second quarter, and he told me to go in for so-and-so. Of course, I didn't know any of the players, so I went to the scorer's table and asked them, 'What's her number?' But it was great. I ended up scoring forty-one points, and after it was over the coach said, 'Jean,

I think we could use you.'" She finished the season high scorer for the team, averaging more than 30 points a game.

After getting her degree at Georgia, she spent the summer playing softball in Satellite Beach, Florida, where she was an All American, and the team ended up second in the nation. Her next job took her to West Virginia Wesleyan in Buckhannon, but because there wasn't a women's AAU team in the area, she found a team in Cincinnati, some 300 miles away. So she'd work at the university during the day and drive to Cincinnati for a game at night.

"I commuted from Buckhannon to Cincinnati in the winter, which was pretty horrible because of the snow and ice and all of that," she said. So to cut the commute, she got a job as teacher and basketball coach at the College of Mt. St. Joseph in Cincinnati in 1971. At the same time she continued to play AAU basketball and softball in Cincinnati. Even though they had a sponsor [Shillito's department store], the basketball players were footing most of the bills. But it was an opportunity to play.

"All they [Shillito's] got us were our uniforms. We had to pay for our food, our shoes, our hotel, whatever we did. Softball, it was the same way. We loved it so much. Just about everybody I know that comes from my era who was involved in sports, they played for the pure enjoyment of the game, to have the opportunity to be good and to be challenged and be competitive.

"When I was elected to the Hall of Fame in Western Carolina, I accepted that award on behalf of all the other athletes. So many of them I thought were good and should have had that chance, but they never would get it."

So remember, Jean is playing basketball and softball, while teaching and coaching at Mt. St. Joe. Her first year there was the first year Ohio had a state Intercollegiate Basketball Championship. Jean's team won. Eventually, she moved to the athletic department's office in 1978. By the time she retired from the Mount, she had a 350-167 career record, was voted to the Greater Cincinnati Basketball Hall of Fame, won the Lifetime Achievement Award from the Ohio Pro/Am Awards in 1997, and had the Mt. St. Joseph gymnasium named the "Jean Dowell Building."

"At Mt. St. Joe we were an all-women's school, so we couldn't say, 'Well, you're doing this for the men, so you must do it for the women.' But we would go to play at other schools, and a lot of big universities would play in what they called the women's gym. It was nothing compared to the arena where the men were playing. Everybody could see that discrimination there. It was so unjust. And we were always saying something about it."

Jean certainly had an opportunity to say something about it in the 1970s, with a last-minute speaking engagement at the University of Cincinnati for a sports medicine symposium. Then-Reds manager Sparky Anderson was supposed to speak on the second night but cancelled at the last minute. Jean agreed to step in and attended the first night to get an idea of the topics.

"I listened to an athletics trainer/physical therapist speak on common injuries to athletes. To paraphrase his remarks, he said, 'Female athletes are weak. They lack the discipline to do what is necessary to get into peak condition. Girls, he said, do not go to the weight room and work out as the boys do. Girls will not run the long distances and do the wind sprints in order to develop the solid base of conditioning needed to be strong in sport.

"'Boys take sports more seriously,' he continued. 'Girls consider sports a social function. They often fall; they giggle; and, win or lose, they are happy to share punch and cookies with their teammates and opponents after the game.' Many people laughed," Jean remembered. "Women, who made up half or more of the group of 300 people, seemed somewhat embarrassed, but they also seemed to accept what the man said."

All of a sudden, Jean had her topic for the next day. "I was gracious in my opening remarks, then said, 'Contrary to what some people believe, girls and women are very capable of strenuous conditioning programs. It is hard work and demanding; however, the female athlete will rise to the challenge and will be as dedicated to the regimen as the male athlete.'"

Jean continued: "I wonder how many times the male athlete would go to the weight room, how many laps he would run, how much enthusiasm he would put into his sprints and his drills if only occasionally, if ever, he got to use the facilities in the school and community; if he had to play the game in an ill-fitting pinny [jersey] instead of a uniform; if only a half-dozen people watched him play or even knew he was playing; if there was no press coverage; if there were no opportunities to win any awards or gain any recognition."

And then, the conclusion: "Schools have given boys knowledgeable coaches and paid them to do the job. They have given them the best facilities and the resources to get the job done. For the girls, the coach is often a mere chaperone volunteering his or her time. In practically all cases, the girls have little use of the facilities. Games, if there are any, are scheduled at a time when people cannot attend.

"Girls don't go to the weight rooms because there are no weight rooms for girls. I would like to ask all who have ever laughed at the ineptitude of girls in athletics what they think they would have accomplished under such a system. I salute those girls who have had the fortitude to withstand such a farcical situation. And just maybe they giggled so much to keep from crying."

Over her nearly five decades in sports, Jean has seen the advent of Title IX and the growth of women's and girls' sports. Even in retirement, she continues to campaign for women's sports, but she knows the work is never done. "I think every chance we get we should take little girls to see college games and high school games, so that they can aspire to do that. If you don't ever have any example, there's no aspiration there.

"I know athletes today, the girls, they don't even realize what has come before them and what people have had to do in order for them to get that chance. As a rule, they kind of think this is the way it's always been, which is OK. It's great and I'm glad they have that opportunity. I hope it just gets bigger and better."

...

While Jean Dowell was starting women's basketball programs at Western Carolina and Georgia, Bernadette Locke was growing up in Tennessee, not knowing she would make history—not only at Georgia, in the program Jean started, but in Division I basketball. It wasn't basketball love at first sight, however—she grew up playing hopscotch and jump rope. In fact, it wasn't until middle school that she became interested in basketball.

"My cousin played basketball and broke the Tennessee [high school] scoring record there. And obviously that sparked my interest as a youngster, watching how my cousin played, just a tremendous basketball player. And I probably started in the seventh grade, started playing late, compared to this day and time when kids start early."

She played basketball in high school, but it wasn't the game most of us are familiar with now. "In high school I played three on three, so going into the college ranks I wanted to learn five on five so I could be a better college player." Coaching at the local junior college was a young student of the game named Andy Landers. "Coach Landers was at Roane State Community College

Bernadette Mattox

at that time and was a tremendous coach. The team was very successful. I felt like I could go there, learn the game of basketball even better, and move on."

She played at Roane State with her twin sister, Juliet, and just as they were about to finish community college, Coach Landers got the opportunity in 1979 to become the first full-time women's coach at the University of Georgia. He took three of his Roane State players, including Bernadette, with him to Athens, where she became Georgia's first female athlete to earn All-American and Academic All-American honors and was in the program's top ten in career assists and steals.

After she graduated Bernadette served as an assistant coach under Landers, starting in 1985, settling into the Lady Bulldog program as recruiting coordinator. Her basketball life was good, her career just getting settled in Athens, when one day she read an article in *USA Today* about Assistant Coach Ralph Willard leaving the University of Kentucky program to take the head coaching job at Western Kentucky University. The story caught her eye because of the quote from then-Wildcat coach Rick Pitino, who said he was thinking about filling the position with a woman.

"I thought, 'Great. He is so innovative.' It was 1989. I said, 'He's thinking ahead, I applaud him, it's great,' put the paper down, never thought anything else about it. Probably a week and a half later, I get a call from Coach Tubby Smith, who was one of Pitino's other assistants, who was helping him lead the search."

Out of a crowd of twenty candidates, Bernadette Locke became the first woman to serve on a Division 1 men's basketball staff, staying in that role for four years. And sure, Coach Pitino knew a good story when he hired one, as he told the *New York Times:* "I liked the idea of naming the first woman assistant because, sure, it got a lot of publicity for us. Name a man to that position and it's on page 36."

But Pitino said that was only a small part of the hire. "She had to be a person who could actually coach, somebody who understood the game from being a top player herself. Also, I felt we needed a different image; there wasn't a heavy emphasis on academics, on career planning, on integrity," he said. "And although she doesn't do our recruiting, she has an impact."

And Bernadette said she had no second thoughts about taking the Kentucky job. "Coach Pitino was an outstanding coach at the time. You knew that he knew basketball, you watched his teams, and to learn from one of the best coaches in the country, what more could you ask for? And I was very fortunate to have the opportunity to be in his ranks and learn a tremendous amount. You're talking about a guy who was innovative at the time. It was amazing the things that I learned from him."

The reaction from the players reflected Coach Pitino's opinion of the hire. "I was there with a group of guys whose parents did a tremendous job raising them. Always respectful, always doing what they were told to do. And again, when it starts from the top, because Coach Pitino respected everything I did, he expected the same things from me as he did his other assistants."

And what a staff of assistants she joined: "Tubby Smith, who was at Georgia, Kentucky, Minnesota; Billy Donovan, who has two national championships at Florida; Herb Sendek at North Carolina State and Arizona State, and I was with those guys. Totally respectful. I think when you make a change like that, and the respect comes from the top, then I think it's going to go well. But the players were totally super, and I've got to commend their parents."

But she wasn't finished breaking barriers yet. In 1995 Bernadette, who was now Bernadette Locke-Mattox, became the fifth head coach and first African-American to coach Kentucky women's basketball, a position she held for eight years, during which she recorded the team's first twenty-win season and a trip to the NCAA Tournament.

She eventually became an assistant with the WNBA's Connecticut Sun, was an assistant for the USA Basketball Women's World Championship team that won a gold medal in 1998, and received the National Junior College Athletic Association's Achievement Award in 2007. But she never forgot the lessons she learned, being the first to lead women into the Division 1 men's coaching ranks.

"You can't be afraid of failure and not being able to achieve. You've got to go after what you want," she said. "I think we're in a day and time in the world where it's OK that women step beyond the boundaries of wanting to do something that maybe they haven't done before that's going to inspire women. Because we're in a time now where I just think anything goes.

"If a woman can step up and lead, and get things done, why not? We're capable, we're strong minded, and I applaud any young woman, young girl, who has high aspirations for herself, who wants to achieve and wants to break the barriers of stepping out of the box.

"I applaud her and my support will be behind her. I think that's how I got to where I am today because of the women before me who had those aspirations. They stepped beyond the boundaries."

chapter 10

Driving Forces

"There are just these stereotypes of what you're supposed to do."
—Kelley Earnhardt,
General Manager, JR Motorsports

One of my first trips to the Indianapolis 500 was in 1977. We were sitting in the bleachers on the inside of the track, right behind the pits, a great place to see all the action. The field included such Indy greats as Johnny Rutherford, Mario Andretti, and the legendary A.J. Foyt. But the one driver I was there to watch was a rookie who started twenty-sixth in the field, driving the Bryant Heating and Cooling Offenhauser, the number 27 of Janet Guthrie, the first woman to drive at the Brickyard. Talk about breaking into the good ol' boys' club! But while Janet was driving in her first Indy 500, by this time she was a veteran race car driver, and a veteran thrill-seeker, a passion she says started in high school and continued at the University of Michigan.

"I always was adventurous, as you might imagine," Janet told me. "By the time I picked out my college, I had already soloed in an airplane, made a parachute jump, and the summer after high school I got my private pilot's license. [Her dad was a pilot for Eastern Air Lines.] And at that time women could not fly airplanes commercially; they could not fly airplanes for the military, and I loved flying. So I wanted to make a living in the best possible venue, and that was aeronautical engineering, and I picked Michigan out of a book for that specialty."

In Ann Arbor, she found that, in the late 1950s, not that many women were planning to be engineers of any kind. "If I remember right," she said, "there were eight women in a freshman engineering class of 2,000. But I'll confess, I only lasted a year of drawing pictures of the threads on screws and mixing up batches of concrete, sand, and gravel, and then I changed to a physics major, which got me into the aerospace industry anyway."

She took the scenic route to get there, though. At the end of Janet's sophomore year at Michigan, she took a year off, earned a commercial pilot's license and flight instructor's rating, then spent a couple of months in Europe. She returned to school, graduated in 1960, and took a job at Republic Aviation in Long Island, New York. Republic was, at the time, opening a new facility for aerospace projects. Her passion for flight now became her profession.

And it almost got her a trip into space, in one of the early civilian astronaut programs. "I gave it my best shot, at the first scientist-astronaut program. They listed the requirements, and I met them all—the pilot's license, the this, the that. They said, Ph.D preferred, and I didn't have a Ph.D., but I did have, at that point, I think, six years of hands-on experience in the aerospace industry, so I gave her a shot. And I have a letter from Deke Slayton that says, 'Thanks for a great try, don't call us, we'll call you.'"

Ironically, it was her love of airplanes and flight that eventually put her behind the wheel of a race car, as she started searching for a plane of her own that she could fly. "I went to look at an AT-6, a World War II training airplane, that was stressed for six G's positive and six G's negative. It was capable of all sorts of wonderful acrobatics. And I thought about all the heavy [air] traffic in the New York area and how hard it would be to go find a place to have fun, and I walked away [from buying it].

"Instead, I bought a seven-year-old Jaguar XK 120, just because it was such a beautiful thing. And then I found out what I could do with it. What they now call autocrosses, the one-car-at-a-time competitions, hillclimbs, and I discovered the whole world of sports car racing."

That opened a whole new world of adventure for Janet, who raced first as an amateur, then professionally, in the sports car circuit. She had two class victories in the twelve hours of Sebring, she was North Atlantic Road Racing champion, drove Trans-Am races, and had successful finishes in nine consecutive runnings of the Daytona 24-hour, Sebring 12-hour, and Watkins Glen 500. She was making a name for herself in the road-racing field.

But road racing was one thing—racing an open-wheel vehicle at the Indianapolis 500 was certainly something else. That was

territory that women drivers had
yet to visit. But in 1976, Janet
got the phone call that would
change her life and change racing
history.

"I owe it all to one of the last
of the shoestring team owners, a
guy named Rolla Vollstedt, from
Portland, Oregon," she said, "A
World War II veteran, a member
of the greatest generation, he
had always been an innovator.
He brought the first successful
American-built car with a rear wing
to Indianapolis and a number of

Janet Guthrie

other innovations. And he just decided he'd like to be the first team
owner to bring a woman driver to Indianapolis, so he called me up.

"And I had never heard of him. He got my answering machine.
And before I returned his call, I called Chris Economaki, the racing
guru and editor of one of the major trade newspapers, *National Speed
Sport News*, and I said, 'Chris, who is Rolla Vollstedt?' And Chris
told me that he was real. So I called him back, and we arranged a
test and went on from there."

The test was at Ontario Motor Speedway outside of Los Angeles,
in a car originally built in 1971. And Janet did it with a broken bone
in her foot, cracked as she was jogging in place a few days earlier.
She turned a lap of more than 172 miles an hour and, as she said in
her book *Janet Guthrie: A Life at Full Throttle*: "But had I known what

my life would be like in the weeks after that fact was made public, I might not have been all that cheerful...None of us, I think—not even Rolla—anticipated what a sensation we were about to create, what a hornet's nest we were stirring up."

Her entry into the 500 was announced March 9, 1976, in Indianapolis. While reaction was pretty straightforward, later in the week came this quote from the *Boston Globe* on March 14: "Concoct, if you will, your own bizarre picture of the Indy start. Have Ms. Guthrie fishing in her three-feet-by-two-feet handbag for her keys, with bobby pins and Max Factor beauty aids and hair brushes and ballpoint pens and clipped newspaper recipes flying through the air. Have her still working on her eyelashes in the rear-view mirror as the other 32 drivers angrily blow their horns."

In the meantime, another female driver, Arlene (Lanzieri) Hiss, whom Janet knew from the Sports Car Club of America, was also aiming to make it to Indianapolis with a start in the Indy car race that March at Phoenix. Janet was there to watch Arlene get lapped within the first ten miles and finish fourteenth, the last of the cars still running. "Drivers of the fastest cars kept finding Arlene on their line," Janet said in her book. "Spins and crashes brought out the yellow repeatedly. Although Arlene was nowhere in the vicinity of any incident, she was black-flagged after the gestures of the other drivers left no doubt as to their sentiments."

Janet added, "It was months before I talked with Arlene. Eventually, I heard that there had been problems with her crew. Between that and the three-ring circus that surrounded her debut, Arlene had lost her composure."

After Arlene's problems, Janet made sure that she had the respect of those around her, to make her Indy debut as smooth as possible. "Let's begin with the crew," Janet said. "It quickly became pretty clear to the guys who worked for Rolla Vollstedt that I knew the mechanics of cars inside and out. I'd been building my own engines and doing my own bodywork for thirteen years. And that helped. And a lot of drivers ignore their crew or look down at them. That is a really big mistake, likely to be a fatal one. As to the drivers, the only way that could be done was on the race track. And that began with my very first Indy car race at the beginning of May 1976."

That was at Trenton Speedway in Trenton, New Jersey, where she was welcomed to the Indy car fraternity by none other than the king of Indy cars, A.J. Foyt. "The most astonishing thing that happened at that first race at Trenton was that A.J. Foyt came down to our pit and said hello to me. And he's shaking hands and telling me I'm doing a good job, and I'm trying to shut my mouth before any flies fly into it, so that was one of the first really big boosts that we had. It didn't all happen immediately, of course, but it did happen."

After Trenton, where she qualified fourteenth and finished fifteenth, it was on to Indianapolis for the month-long effort of practices and testing to qualify for the 1976 Indianapolis 500. At a venue where women weren't even allowed in the pits until 1971 (the rule for most U.S. raceways), her presence caused quite a stir. "The first time I drove out onto the track in practice, I was saying to myself, 'Now listen, it's just like Trenton, only bigger,' and myself said back, 'What, are you kidding me?'

"That very first year, we did the best we could. I did not make a qualifying attempt that year because I couldn't make the car go any faster than a really, really, good experienced driver had been able to make it go the previous year. So I had to wait until 1977 for my first start."

The year was still notable for Janet at Indy, as she was the first woman to be entered there, and to pass the rookie test. She again made history in May of 1976, when she became the first woman to compete in a NASCAR Winston Cup superspeedway event, the Charlotte World 600, where she finished fifteenth out of forty starters. She was easing her way into the top racing circles, but Indianapolis in 1977 was still her goal. That year, and that car, turned out to be a lot better for Janet.

"We had a good car; I set fastest time of day on opening day of practice; I was among the top ten for several days. And then I hit the wall, and that caused us a great deal of grief and aggravation, so I ended up qualifying on the very last day of qualifying, the second weekend." She ended up in the middle of the next-to-last row of the eleven rows of three in 1977, with a qualifying average of 188.403.

You can imagine the media crush that led up to the May 29 race. But one of the biggest questions, and mysteries, was how Speedway owner Tony Hulman would modify his traditional "Gentlemen, start your engines" command. Hulman built the track from a run-down, weed-filled venue, to the pinnacle of motor sports. It turned out to be the last 500 he would attend, as he died in October of that year. Perhaps it was fitting for Hulman's last race, to be the first race for a new era of female drivers.

As he took the microphone that day to start the race, drivers and spectators alike stopped to listen to his historic words. "In company with the first lady ever to qualify at Indianapolis," Hulman commanded, "Gentlemen, start your engines." But at that moment, Janet had a few more things on her mind than the history she was making on the track.

"At the beginning of the race, really, I was just focused on who was around me, what were the characteristics of the drivers behind me, the characteristics of the drivers in front of me, what was the track condition going to be after four days of not having been raced on, with trash blowing around and what not, the infinite little details that enable you to make a success of it."

A timing gear problem knocked Janet out of that first 500, and she finished twenty-ninth and earned $16,556 for her team. But it wasn't the finish that was memorable; it was her start. At first, Janet didn't realize what her presence in the Indy field meant, not just for her, but for women in and out of sports. "I was in this because racing had been a passion and an obsession for me for many years. But gradually I was persuaded by a lot of people that this was meaningful to women in other fields.

"I remember the parade that year [the 500 Festival parade that includes the drivers, traditionally held the Saturday before the race]. I didn't even know there was a parade, but a huge parade with enormous crowds, and there would be guys holding up their little daughters over their heads, as if the guys thought that this was their daughters' future. I was really moved by that and realized I had to try to live up to the responsibility."

Actually, Janet's run in the 1977 Indianapolis 500 wasn't even her first history-making start that year. She was the first woman, and, the top rookie, at the Daytona 500, finishing twelfth. So what was the difference between being accepted at Indy and being accepted by her fellow drivers at Daytona? "In stock cars, which I ran my first stock car race actually in May of '76 [at Charlotte], it did take a little longer for the guys to come around. It was, at that time, still largely, though not entirely, a Southern sport.

"But once the guys realized that driving against me was just like driving against any other driver, things changed. And that was one of the most gratifying things that happened while I was driving."

Janet's best finish at Indy was the following year, in 1978, when she took the Texaco Star to ninth place. Her last appearance in the field of thirty-three was in 1979, and there wasn't another woman in the field for more than a decade, until Lyn St. James drove in the 1992 race. There's a saying in racing, that speed is money—how fast do you want to go? Janet says money was an issue for her and remains an issue for many female drivers.

"That is the hardest part, and in my opinion it is especially difficult for women," Janet said. "Look at Alli Owens, who, in Danica Patrick's inaugural race in stock cars, the ARCA race at Daytona this last February [2010], ran third for a long time. And Danica Patrick, back at the back of the pack in thirty-something, was getting all the attention. [Danica eventually finished sixth in her stock car debut.] Alli doesn't have all that much funding. I wish she did.

"Sarah Fisher, my favorite Indy car driver, doesn't have all that much funding. There are two more drivers who are new to Indianapolis this year. Simona De Silvestro, who is Swiss, and Ana Beatriz, who is Brazilian, and they have both been doing quite, quite well in practice. It just depends on who gets the chance, what their talent is, and whether they can find the funding."

What a difference thirty-three years have made at the Brickyard. From Janet Guthrie becoming the first woman to run at Indy, fast forward to 2010, where in the Indianapolis 500 field, Beatriz started on the outside of Row 7, De Silvestro on the inside of Row 8, Patrick in the middle of Row 8, and Fisher, the middle of Row 10, marking the first time four women had been in the 500 starting field. And with a touch of irony, Fisher has been mentored by four-time Indy winner Al Unser Sr., who went very public with his criticism of Janet Guthrie's 1977 Indy start. Fisher lists him as one of her driving heroes, along with Guthrie. Janet Guthrie made history and paved the way for other women drivers to be accepted, by doing what she loved to do. She gives the same advice to others:

"I tend to say, go where your passion is. And also, go where your talent is. I do a lot of motivational speaking as you might imagine, and many motivational speakers are always saying, 'Well, you can do anything you set your mind to.' That's not actually true. You have to have A, the talent, and B, the desire. And if you put those things together, indeed, a young woman can do anything she wants to. And more now, I think, than thirty-three years ago."

...

For Kelley Earnhardt, racing is personal.

It has been, ever since she grew up in the heart of North Carolina, in the heart of NASCAR racing, as the daughter of the legendary, seven-time Winston Cup champion Dale Earnhardt.

Racing lends itself to being a family sport, from working on cars in the family garage during the week, to packing up the kids and watching the locals battle it out on the county dirt track. NASCAR

Kelley Earnhardt

has its share of celebrated families, from the Pettys to the Allisons to the Waltrips and Bodines. But no family holds the aura and the interest of race fans like the Earnhardts. And no one guides the business of the next Earnhardt racing generation like Kelley.

She didn't start out as a business whiz, though; she started out thinking she might follow her father in racing. "I chose to get through high school and move on to college and get my degree. I had been down in Wilmington, North Carolina, for about three years and really didn't come home a lot during that time. My dad wrote me one day, actually sent me flowers, and said, 'It's been so long since I've seen you, I've almost forgotten what you look like.'

"We got to talking and he said, 'I really would like you to move home and finish school in Charlotte, and if you want to race, I'll start you racing.' So I moved back home in 1993, and I started racing street stocks at that point. And then I moved to late models in '94, '95, and '96 with my brothers Kerry and Dale. We ran the Saturday night short tracks around North Carolina and Virginia and South Carolina, some other places. I drove for three years and really, really enjoyed it."

In fact, some thought that of the three Earnhardt siblings, Kelley had the most potential in the business. Mark Dyer, a former

NASCAR executive, told *USA Today*, "I watched her race, and she could more than hold her own with Kerry and Dale Jr. At the time, a lot of people felt she was the best prospect of the three."

Even Dale Jr. thought that Kelley could make a profession behind the wheel. He told ESPN, "She could have had a lot of opportunities had it been a different environment and a different culture and a different climate. She was hardheaded and tough and drove hard. She would eventually have polished her abilities to where she would have been a pretty good race car driver at the higher level."

Kelley realized what the differences meant, though: "The sport in the mid-1990s, it wasn't welcoming to women," she said in the same interview.

Tony Eury Jr., her cousin and crew chief for JR Motorsports, recognized her talent. "She was very good at what she did," said Eury. "I raced her several times over at Tri-County [Racetrack in Brasstown, North Carolina]. We thought she probably had as much or more talent than any of them [the Earnhardt siblings]."

So while Kerry, the oldest son of Dale Sr., and Dale Jr. made it to NASCAR's various divisions, Kelley headed to the business side of the sport. "Back then, it was certainly a different place for women in our sport—a lot more barriers for us to overcome," she said. "And at that point, I had just graduated from college in '95, and I was working for Sports Image, the company my dad had purchased that made licensed products, T-shirts, hats, and that kind of stuff. I was doing really well there and enjoying it, and I was leaving on Fridays and going to race. And our sponsorship came up for our late model cars, and my brothers both worked in the shop, so it was kind of natural. They just kept working on their cars and doing their thing, and I was just kind of left with the decision to move on, because there wasn't sponsorship for the cars to run. So it just kind of fizzled out, and I stayed true on my business course and continued to work for Sports Image."

In fact, the experience at Sports Image, her father's company, helped give her the experience she would need in eventually taking over her brother's racing business. Dale Earnhardt Sr. and his then-wife, Teresa, were the first to realize the marketing power of the Earnhardt name, the "Intimidator" moniker, and the number 3 car. They trademarked Dale's image and signature and created a business template that almost every racing team follows today. While Kelley worked on the marketing end of the team, Dale Jr. joined his father at DEI, and the kids seemed settled in the family business.

Everything changed, though, on February 18, 2001. On the final lap of the Daytona 500, Dale Earnhardt's car made contact with Sterling Marlin's and hit the wall at Turn 4. Earnhardt was pronounced dead that evening at nearby Halifax Hospital. The patriarch of Dale Earnhardt Incorporated (DEI) was gone, even though the business of Dale Earnhardt continued. And it led to some tough decisions made by Kelley and her brother.

"It was August of 2001, about six months after we lost our dad," she said. "Before, when my dad was alive, at Dale Earnhardt Incorporated, whatever was good for Dad, was good for Dale Jr. Whatever insurance they had, or whatever deals they were doing, they worked Dale into, so they kind of carried Dale's business as he was getting started in racing in '98. So I was working at Action

Performance, which had bought Sports Image, and I just felt I was in a really difficult position. Because I was constantly in meetings about how much Dale Earnhardt product we were going to make, what this was going to do for us and what that was going to do for us, and it got really hard to be in those kinds of meetings.

"So I called Dale and I said, 'You know, I need to do something different, and you need somebody to help you' because at that point without Dad being there—he was kind of the glue that put everything together—I said, 'You need somebody to come over and oversee what you have going on.'

"He said, 'Well, Kelley, you make a lot of money, you make way too much money, I can't afford you.' And I said, 'I'm willing to talk about that.' We laugh about it now, because he said, 'You're going to probably have to take a 50 to 60 percent pay cut,' which I did, but I was young, and I had what I needed. It wasn't a big deal for me as long as I could pay a house payment and a car payment.

"So that's kind of how it started. I started working for him. I really kind of came in, getting the pieces together. He had very few employees, just basically a secretary that paid his bills and kept up with stuff like that. So I came in and started getting things organized with his investments and insurance and eventually worked into the DEI system with marketing and licensing and working on his Web site.

"We worked on his contract when we re-signed (with DEI) in 2004, and then when we started thinking about whether we were going to stay there after our second contract was up, we started adding more pieces to the business here at JR Motorsports. By that time we had started our own racing, so we were running the race team, then started thinking about handling Dale's licensing ourselves because it was still handled by Dale Earnhardt Incorporated."

In the middle of all this, Dale Jr. announced in early 2007 that he would be leaving DEI, the only Cup racing home he had ever known, at the end of that season. His announcement made him one of the most sought-after free-agent drivers ever. He eventually left his number 8 behind to drive the number 88 [to the great relief of fans who had a tattoo of his old number] of Rick Hendrick and Hendrick Motorsports. While Dale Jr. was driving for Hendrick in NASCAR's top division, he and his sister were building their own racing team, with Dale Jr. owning, and driving, his own car in the next division down, the Nationwide Series.

"So that's how it all evolved, and now here we are with eighty some employees at JR Motorsports, and our two Nationwide teams, and we're still handling all the day to day and ins and outs of Dale's career with marketing and licensing and all that."

Behind it all, Kelley Earnhardt has made the deals, working with sponsors, crew chiefs, and, yes, other owners and managers to help Dale Jr. succeed. So has she gotten any resistance being a female in a testosterone-driven sport?

"Not really," she said, "I can't say that I've experienced that. Maybe my last name helps me in that regard, and I don't get that kind of flack, or maybe they talk about me behind my back, I don't know. But I think that I'm confident that I handle myself well and I'm intelligent, so when I go into the room with all these guys, I'm respected."

And the girl who was out-driving the guys on the North Carolina dirt tracks was now in the position to help another young female driver break in on the NASCAR circuit, albeit one who already had one Indy Car victory and millions of dollars in sponsorship: Danica Patrick. But think about it—a decade earlier it might have been Kelley herself, instead of Danica, joining the Nationwide circuit.

"I don't know if I could have been her because she certainly has a great career on the IRL side, but I had a shot," Kelley said. "But I'm excited to have a capable female in NASCAR, somebody that's proven themselves on the IRL side. We know she can power a race car, and she's got unbelievable marketing potential, which is fantastic for us.

"But I'm really excited about seeing her do well on the track and what that means for the sport. Because it just opens up a whole lot of doors if there's a female driver that can open up a whole lot more doors for sponsorship opportunities. There's a lot of product out there that can be endorsed by a female and can work for companies. And there's a lot of fans out there that we can gain, from the little girls, all the way up. So if you can get more women interested in the sport, that excites me."

Kelley's interest in the sport has helped her carry on a legendary racing name while honoring the legacy of her father. She is now an equal owner at JR Motorsports as she oversees the entire management team, as well as running the family-side businesses such as Hammerhead Entertainment production company, DEJ Realty, and Dale Jr.'s Whisky River restaurants.

Among her awards: She's earned the Top 25 Women in Business Achievement Award from the *Charlotte Business Journal*; in an Associated Press article in April 2007 she was called one of the "most powerful people in the sport of NASCAR," and in

February 2010 was named the Opportunity Award winner by former Indy Car driver Lyn St. James' Women in the Winner's Circle Foundation for bringing Danica Patrick to NASCAR. Having a family legacy is one thing; having the drive to make your passion succeed is another: "I think, in everything that you do, you have to put your best foot forward, and you have to show off your abilities wherever you can and have confidence in yourself. Having that 'I know I can do it' attitude goes a long way, because you put yourself in a lot more situations that you may not have, if you're not confident about it.

"That's what a person can do, and I think there are a lot of things that parents can do and people around them can do. I think there's such a disparity between how you raise your boy and how you raise your girl. You raise your girl to be soft and sweet, and I think if you stand back and look at yourself as parents, and if the things you say to your boy are different than what you'd say to your girl, if we really look at it, I think we hold girls back a lot of times because we're raising them that way.

"There are just these stereotypes of what you're supposed to do, and I think women could get a lot farther if they were raised in a different direction. I think you should give them the tools to do at the same level. So many people have that stereotype that this is what women do, and this is what men do. 'You shouldn't like race cars, you're a girl.' I think having support from family and friends for something that a female wants to do, that goes so much farther."

chapter 11

Playing Ball With the Boys:
The Next Generation

"I think I'm a total product of Title IX—I'm a Title IX baby."

—Rebecca Lobo, ESPN basketball analyst

$\mathcal{S}$ ince the passing of Title IX in 1972, the numbers of girls participating in sports, especially at the high school level, has grown exponentially. For example, just six years after Title IX was enacted, the percentage of girls playing team sports exploded, from about 4 percent to 25 percent. We've all heard the stats that girls who participate in sports are less likely to become pregnant, less likely to use drugs, more likely to be active later in life and the like. But being able to play sports has helped girls and young women cultivate that interest into careers in sports. Partner that with the explosive growth of sports marketing and sports administration programs at the college and university level, and you have a generation growing up with unprecedented opportunities in athletics.

Two such women are Rebecca Lobo and Ruth Riley, both of whom grew up playing basketball, were successful at the highest levels in college, and have made sports, in one way or the other, their careers. They don't know a world without these opportunities.

Rebecca was there to put the University of Connecticut women's basketball program on the map, helping the team win its first national championship in 1995. She won the Naismith and Wade Player of the Year awards, was the Associated Press Female Athlete of the Year, and in 1996 was the youngest member of the gold medal-winning USA women's basketball team at the Olympic Games.

She became one of the marketing faces of the WNBA when it launched in 1997, and she played with the New York Liberty and Connecticut Sun during her seven-year career. She parlayed her basketball expertise into a career at ESPN as basketball analyst and reporter.

"I think I'm a total product of Title IX—I'm a Title IX baby," Rebecca said. I'm really fortunate that I had a mom who was ahead of the curve. She knew about Title IX early on, and when she didn't see me getting the opportunities, she would bring it up. And she would make sure that I had a chance to do the things that I wanted to do.

"When I signed up for basketball, I think it was in the third grade, in my town in the rec league, and the phone call came that I wasn't going to be able to play basketball that year because only two girls signed up, my mom was the one who stepped forward and said,

Rebecca Lobo

'Well, no, that just means that you have to let Rebecca play on the all-boys team.' And so I did."

But not everyone was as excited to have Rebecca playing with the boys. "On that third grade team when I was the only girl, and we would go to play other teams that were made up of all boys, you could see the look on the boys' faces on the other teams like, 'Oh, we don't want to play against a girl.'

"But my teammates were great. The boys on my team were great because all they wanted to do was win. So I was pretty good, and they were happy to have me on their team. But that was the only time where I can remember people treating me a little bit differently because I was a girl."

Playing basketball in the third grade was nothing new for Rebecca, the youngest of three children growing up in New England. "My oldest brother is six-and-a-half years older than I am, and he was always playing sports, and so my sister and I were kind of the tagalong annoying little sisters who just pretty much wanted to do everything that he did. So when he was playing Nerf football, we would try to do that with his friends.

"Then he started playing basketball, and my parents put a basketball hoop up in our driveway, and I kind of fell in love with the game when I was really, really little. I would just go outside and dribble the ball around and try to shoot baskets. I was the little tomboy who played with the boys at recess and played with my brother's friends and just always wanted to be doing something that had to do with sports."

And it didn't take Rebecca long to figure out that she was pretty good at basketball. "I started playing on basketball teams when I was in about the third grade, and I always did pretty well. But it wasn't until I went to my first basketball camp, which I think was right before I went into sixth grade, that summer, that there were coaches who were telling me, 'You're pretty good, and if you keep practicing and working hard, you might be able to go to college on a scholarship.' So that was the first time that I really realized that there was a future other than just playing in the driveway."

That future has taken Rebecca from the driveway to around the globe, playing the game she loves. But the sport also has given her a sense of responsibility and giving back, a vision she shares with her mother. "My mother was diagnosed with breast cancer when I was a junior in college at the University of Connecticut, back in 1993. She and I started a scholarship at the University of Connecticut in 2001 for people going into the allied health sciences and nursing, and for under-represented groups, especially Hispanics. Because they are under-represented in all the health care professions, we think it's really important for those groups, primarily, to get a little bit of extra help. So we started that scholarship, the RuthAnn and Rebecca Lobo Scholarship in Allied Health and Nursing at Connecticut."

She and her mother also have written a book, *The Home Team*, about Rebecca's career and RuthAnn's cancer battle. It's teamwork that started when RuthAnn made sure that Rebecca got to play with the boys on her third grade team. "I had a great advocate in the home and a woman who was very aware of Title IX," said Rebecca. "And as I went through, if things weren't being enforced, she brought it up. So much of my success, most of my success, is a result of opportunities that became available because of Title IX."

. . .

The story is similar for Ruth Riley, who was born in Kansas but grew up in the heartland of basketball-mad Indiana. In her official bio, Ruth says she was 25 inches long at birth, "and never looked back from there." She also admits she was made fun of as a kid, because she was so lanky and shy. Basketball came later and became her passion. Eventually recruited by Muffet McGraw at Notre Dame, she helped the Irish win the NCAA Championship in 2001, and she was named the NCAA Finals Most Valuable Player. That same year she was named the Naismith Player of the Year and the Big East Player of the Year.

She was drafted into the WNBA that spring and eventually picked up two WNBA titles in Detroit and was the 2003 WNBA Finals Most Valuable Player. She also won a gold medal in 2004 with the USA women's basketball team. In addition, she travels extensively throughout the world for her causes, the "Nothing But Nets" program for mosquito nets to fight malaria and the TRIAD Trust for AIDS education. The opportunity that Ruth received to play basketball as a child has opened doors for her as an adult to serve around the world.

"First I'm grateful [for Title IX]," said Ruth. "My mom is my role model, and the opportunities she didn't have and wished she had made me appreciate more the fact that I had them growing up, and I had the opportunities to pursue what I was passionate about."

And she was passionate about sports, from a young age. "I was never that good growing up, but I loved to play. Coordination came a little later, but I've always loved sports, and growing up in a small country town in Indiana [Macy], if you played one sport you're going to play them all, just because you need somebody to fill out the rosters there. But basketball was definitely my passion."

And that meant that, sometimes, she was the only girl playing with the boys. "I don't know if they wanted me, but I was always there when I was growing up. I think it's tremendous now that we have so many young girls that play, so maybe it's different now, but if I went to the gym, I was the only girl there.

"So it wasn't me choosing to play with the boys over the girls, it was just there were these guys who were there. And I had some older cousins who took me under their wing, and when they would go play pickup, they would take me with them.

"And you learn quickly that when you play with the guys, they're not going to pass you the ball twice if you mess up the first time. And they don't really put the hand out to pick you up after they knock you down. But I think I learned a lot and gained their respect along the way."

She also gives a lot of credit to her mother, Sharon Riley, who raised the three Riley youngsters on her own. "First, she encouraged me to dream," Ruth said, "to dream big, to realize that I'm able to accomplish things that I set my mind to. But then she made sure that I knew that I had to work really hard to reach my goals. I think the examples that she set with her work ethic and the sacrifices she made to raise us on her own, I'm just grateful.

Ruth Riley

"She showed me personally throughout my life what it takes to be successful, though success for her is not defined by basketball. It's defined by the family that she raised and what she was able to accomplish personally."

To that end, Mom was probably pretty proud of Ruth when she took on the role of coach in a charity basketball game in 2009 back in Ashland, Kansas, on the other side of Dodge City from Ransom, Kansas, where Ruth was born. The occasion was an all-star charity women's basketball game to raise money to make cancer screening services more available for people in that area. The catalyst was Southwest Missouri State's Jackie Stiles, the NCAA all-time leading scorer, who's from another small Kansas town, Claflin.

"During the Final Four and throughout college, I played on some U.S. teams where I got to know Jackie Stiles," Ruth said. "She called me and asked if I could coach in the game, and I said I'd love to. So my coaching debut was against Hall of Famer Cynthia Cooper, one of the best players to ever play our game."

The game drew a sellout crowd of 1,000, plus an overflow crowd watching on a big screen at the high school stadium. "It was an amazing event. It's just a great reminder of community in these five small communities in western Kansas, just coming together to raise money not only for breast health awareness, but to take care of the women in the community. I love playing basketball, but to be able to use the sport to make a difference in people's lives, I think that's what I'm passionate about as well."

Her passion for giving back is a responsibility that Ruth feels she owes the sport. "I feel like our sport transcends a lot of barriers, and whether it's here, or internationally when I travel to Africa, I may not be able to speak the same language, but somehow we're able to communicate just because of my relationship with sports.

"And with that opportunity, I'm given a platform that I can use for good, or not use at all. I embrace that opportunity. I feel like I have the opportunity to do that, and do something good, whether it's here, talking to young girls and inspiring them to believe in themselves, or whether it's overseas, the work that I do with the United Nations Foundation with their malaria initiative or with the HIV work I do in Africa as well."

When she talks with young girls, she has some specific messages for them. "Dare to dream. The possibilities are endless. But believing in yourself is key, especially for young girls. Really believe in yourself. Don't let somebody take your self-confidence or self-worth from you. And work extremely hard, because nothing is given easily. So dream big, believe in yourself, and definitely work hard."

This is from a young girl who admits on her bio that she started her basketball career spending more time on the bench than on the court in junior high, who was the last one to get into the games during her freshman year at Notre Dame, who made the most of her opportunity to play basketball as a youngster, and who now uses the game to do good around the world.

"It's something I don't take for granted. I think that it's great now that girls have basketball programs that they can enter into at just about any age, multi-level programs during the summer and during school. And I think it's an exciting time to be a youth, to be a young girl and have dreams and want to pursue them because they have the opportunities to do that."

afterword

Maureen Hester, Shelly Bellman, and Shannon Lynes don't know a world where girls and women didn't have the opportunity to play sports.

Maureen was a star at Bethel Park High School in the Pittsburgh area, earning Freshman of the Year honors in the league and scoring nearly 1,150 points in her career. A first-team Ohio basketball All-State and three-time All-League and All-District selection in high school, Shelly was born two years after Billie Jean King retired from tennis and fourteen years after the passage of Title IX. In Maryland, Shannon scored fifty-two goals in her senior year of lacrosse at River Hill, in a state where lacrosse is king, and she was named second team All-County as a high school junior and senior.

Maureen's team, the Xavier Musketeers, made it to the Elite Eight her senior season. After knee injuries threatened to cut her collegiate career short, Shelly was able to petition for, and receive, a sixth year of basketball eligibility. In Shannon's case, it wasn't injury that threatened to end her college career—it was, in an ironic twist, Title IX.

"As long as I can remember, I've wanted to play basketball," said Maureen. I can't think of a time when I wasn't allowed to play, even if I was the only girl there. It was just accepted. If there wasn't a girls' team, I'd play with the boys' team.

For Shelly, not having equal access to equipment and facilities isn't even imaginable. "We hear stories about 'back in the day,' the women's basketball team would have to practice and play in the gym that's downstairs, a beat-up gym, because the boys had the main gym," said Shelly. "I'd hear those stories but could not imagine it. And their jerseys, their practice jerseys were hand-me-downs from years and years and years ago. And now we get practice jerseys new every year. We get new game jerseys every year. We get new basketball shoes every year. I don't think we really realize what it was like before Title IX."

Shannon was able to earn a lacrosse scholarship to Ohio University, where she played in ten games as a freshman. But being able to continue her college career wasn't so easy after that. "When I first entered college, I do not believe I fully understood what Title IX meant," said Shannon. "What I did understand was there were certain standards the university had to meet as far as opportunities for men and women were concerned. But just two weeks before the lacrosse season started my sophomore year of college [in 2007], my world seemed to come crashing down.

"Practice was suddenly cancelled with no reason, and a mandatory meeting was scheduled for that afternoon. In addition, the men's swimming, men's indoor track, and men's cross country all received notice of a mandatory team meeting. When 5:00 p.m. came, Athletic Director Kirby Hocutt walked into our lacrosse room and informed us the university would no longer offer women's lacrosse as a Division I sport. Title IX was cited as a main reason." [By eliminating the lacrosse program, the percentage of the school's female student-athletes became more in proportion to the percentage of women attending the school. The aforementioned men's programs also were cut as the university tried to reduce a budget deficit of more than $4 million.]

Shannon eventually transferred to the University of Cincinnati, where she was the team captain for the lacrosse program's inaugural season. "While the sport I loved was cut from the school I was attending, I had the option to transfer to another university that would give me an opportunity to compete in the sport I love. Not only because of the joy of playing the game, but also the unity and bonds I have created as a result of being part of a team. I will be forever grateful for the sacrifices the women before me have made."

Three athletes—three perspectives of the opportunities now afforded young girls and women in sports. Whatever the perspective, at least the opportunities are there. And it is because of the work, the compassion, and the passion of many of these women profiled here, that Maureen, Shelly, and Shannon can't imagine a world where they're not allowed to 'play ball with the boys.'

sources

Chapter 2

Allida Black, ed., *The Eleanor Roosevelt Papers: Volume I,* Scribners, 2007.

AWSMonline.org.

Frank Deford, "Sometimes the Bear Eats You," *Sports Illustrated,* March 29, 2010.

Linda K. Fuller, *Sportscasters/Sportscasting: Principles and Practices,* Routledge, 2008.

Dave Kaszuba, "Bringing Women to the Sports Pages: Margaret Goss and the 1920s," *American Journalism,* Volume 23 (Spring 2006).

Billie Jean King with Christine Brennan, *Pressure Is a Privilege: Lessons I've Learned from Life and the Battle of the Sexes,* LifeTime Media, Inc., 2008.

Billie Jean King interview, Fox19 Sports, WXIX-TV, Cincinnati.

Maryland Women's Hall of Fame.

Claire Noland, "Pioneering Sports Journalist" (Mary Garber obituary), *Los Angeles Times*, September 24, 2008.

Chapter 3

Brian T. Horowitz, "So What Do You Do, Lesley Visser?," www.mediabistro.com, January 27, 2010.

Rudy Martzke, "Aiming for More Air Time," *USA Today*, September 7, 2000.

Kerry Monaco, "Liguori Is a Groundbreaker for Women," *Southampton Press*, 2006. www.sportsonline.com, "Sports News You Can Use: Television Sportscasters".

Chapter 4

Bill Marx, "Sierens Proves the Skeptics Wrong," *Orlando Sentinel*, December 28, 1987.

Richard Sandomir, "First Woman to Call N.F.L. Play-by-Play, and the Last," *New York Times*, January 29, 2009.

Jim Sarni, "NBC Will Let Woman Call NFL," *Orlando Sentinel*, October 31, 1987.

Jack Smith, "Being Football Fan Eases Way for Her Play-by-Play," *Seattle Post-Intelligencer*, December 22, 1987.

Chapter 5

Christine Brennan, *Best Seat in the House,* Scribner, 2006.

John Koblin, "Who's This Lady? Meet Selena Roberts, A-Rod's Worst Nightmare," *New York Observer*, February 10, 2009.

Selena Roberts, *A-Rod: The Many Lives of Alex Rodriguez,* Harper, 2009.

Selena Roberts and David Epstein, "Confronting A-Rod," *Sports Illustrated*, February 16, 2009.

"Alex Rodriguez Press Conference: Steroid Use Discussed," *Huffington Post*, February 17, 2009.

Chapter 6

Tim Brown, "Can Kim Ng Break the Gender Barrier?" Yahoo! Sports, July 3, 2008. Tony Jackson, "Executive Decisions," ESPN.com, January 22, 2010.

Chapter 7

Jonathan Berr, "Media World: Ranks of Women Fantasy Football Players Growing," dailyfinance.com, August 13, 2009.

Jason Franchuk, "Vegas Bowl Director a Bundle of Energy," *Daily Herald*, Provo, Utah, December 21, 2006.

Brian Hilderbrand and Ron Kantowski, "Take Five: Pioneer Las Vegas Bowl," *Las Vegas Sun*, December 24, 2007.

Adam Kiefaber, "KHSAA's Brigid DeVries to Retire," Coachesaid.com, December 16, 2009.

Liza Porteus Viana, *Putting Her Best Foot Forward*, Portfolio.com, December 28, 2007.

Jeff Wolf, "Pair Entering Local Hall Praise Others for Honor," *Las Vegas Review Journal*, June 8, 2007.

"Woman to lead athletic group," *Cincinnati Enquirer*, May 16, 2002.

Chapter 8

Virginia Lopez, "It Took a Village to Grow This Champion," Womenssportsnet.com.

"Sue Enquist Retires as UCLA's Head Softball Coach Effective January 1," www.uclabruins.com, September 26, 2006.

Jon Show, "Changes Move LPGA Events Closer to Renewals," *Sports Business Journal*, August 24, 2009

Beth Ann Baldry, "A Closer Look at the 2010 LPGA Schedule," *Golfweek,* Nov. 18, 2009.

Chapter 9

Robin Finn, "College Basketball: An Aide With a Different Image," *New York Times,* December 20, 1992.

Timothy W. Smith, "At Kentucky, Tradition Takes a Twist," *New York Times,* November 18, 1997.

Mike Szostak, "Women Coaching Men: Former Pitino Assistant Says Her Time at Kentucky Was 'A Great Experience,'" *Providence Journal,* July 22, 2009.

Staff, "Mattox, McDaniel are Roane State's Outstanding Alumni for 2007," *Crossville Chronicle,* October 22, 2007.

Chapter 10

Janet Guthrie, *Janet Guthrie: A Life at Full Throttle,* SportClassic Books, 2005.

David Newton, "Junior Took a Backseat to Big Sis Kelley," ESPN. com, January 26, 2010.

Nate Ryan, "Kelley Earnhardt Reflects on a Career that Might Have Been," *USA Today,* December 15, 2009.

Chapter 11

Tara Parker-Pope, "As Girls Become Women, Sports Pay Dividends," *New York Times,* February 15, 2010.

Joe Posnanski, "Small Town, Big Game," *Sports Illustrated,* November 9, 2009. www.rebeccalobo.com.

www.ruthriley.com.

Afterword

Mark Znidar, "Running on Empty: Ohio University's Decision to Ax Track and Field Leaves Athletes Hurt, Disillusioned," *Columbus Dispatch*, May 3, 2007.

Interviews throughout the book courtesy of 91.7 WVXU, Cincinnati, *The Front Row*: Tonya Antonucci; Christine Brennan; Kelley Earnhardt; Janet Guthrie; Ann Liguori; Rebecca Lobo; Bernadette Mattox; Kim Ng; Ruth Riley; Selena Roberts; Gayle Sierens; Lesley Visser; Pam Ward.

photo credits

We gratefully acknowledge the following sources of the photos that appear in this book:

Billie Jean King: Courtesy Michael E. Anderson

T. Jean Howell: Courtesy T. Jean Howell

Dr. Michelle Andrews: Courtesy Donna Poehner/Zia Portrait Design

Tina Kunzer-Murphy: Courtesy John Gurzinski/*Las Vegas Review-Journal*

Selena Roberts: Courtesy Karen Wall Bush

Kelley Earnhardt: Courtesy Harold Hinson Photography

Ann Liguori: Courtesy Ann Liguori

Bernadette Mattox: Courtesy Connecticut Sun

Tonya Antonucci: Courtesy Women's Professional Soccer

Rebecca Lobo: Courtesy ESPN

Pam Ward: Courtesy ESPN

Janet Guthrie: Courtesy Motorsports Images and Archives for Talladega Superspeedway

Ruth Riley: Courtesy Mike Bennett

Brigid DeVries: Courtesy Kentucky High School Athletic Association

Christine Brennan: Courtesy Lisa Williams

Lesley Visser: Courtesy AP Images

Kari Rumsfield: Courtesy Donna Poehner/Zia Portrait Design

Gayle Sierens: Courtesy WFLA-TV

Zayra Calderon: Courtesy LPGA

Sue Enquist: Courtesy UCLA

Photos of Betsy Ross: courtesy Harold Kramer Photography and KPG Creative (with headset); courtesy of Neysa Ruhl Photography (author photo).

Betsy Ross was one of the first women to break into national sports media when she worked as an anchor on ESPN's *SportsCenter* in the late 1990s. She held the position for five years. She currently is president and founder of Game Day Communications. Before anchoring *SportsCenter* and ESPN News, Ross worked at NBC News Channel and Cincinnati's NBC affiliate, WLWT-TV, for seven years.

She continues to be involved in sports broadcasting as play-by-play anchor for women's college basketball for ESPN, Fox Sports, and other national and regional outlets, and as a sports reporter for Cincinnati's FOX 19. She is the host of a weekly sports interview segment, "The Front Row," that airs Saturday mornings on WVXU-FM, the NPR affiliate in Cincinnati. She also teaches a master's level course, Sports and PR, at Xavier University. She is active in a variety of organizations, including the Special Olympics, and the Greater Cincinnati-Northern Kentucky Women's Sports Association.

Ross is a native of Connersville, Indiana, and received her bachelor's degree at Ball State University and master's degree at the University of Notre Dame. She is on the board of the Ball State University Foundation. She has received the Sagamore of the Wabash award, the highest civilian award given to Indiana residents, and is a Kentucky Colonel.

CPSIA information can be obtained
at www.ICGtesting.com
Printed in the USA
LVHW022331040219
606388LV00003B/5/P